Touching Stones

Turning Tables

&

Crying in the Rain

*Stories from a Journey to
Beloved Community*

MARQUE M JENSEN

© 2013 Marque Jensen
All Rights Reserved.

No part of this publication may be reproduced, stored in a retrieval system, or transmitted, in any form or by any means, electronic, mechanical, photocopying, recording, or otherwise, without the written permission of the author.

First published by Dog Ear Publishing
4010 W. 86th Street, Ste H
Indianapolis, IN 46268
www.dogearpublishing.net

dog ear
PUBLISHING

ISBN: 978-1-4575-2208-6

This book is printed on acid-free paper.

Printed in the United States of America

Contents

To the reader vi

Acknowledgements viii

INTRODUCTION 1

Full Circle, Under a Full Moon, on a Sledding Hill 2

The Human Race 8

A Journey to Solidarity and Credibility 9

The Gift of Perspective across Culture 10

The Call to RISK beyond Race and Class 13

THE BEAUTY OF A COMMUNITY FILLED WITH DIVERSITY ... 17

An Awareness of Incompleteness 18

The Cost of Relationships that reflect Heaven 22

The Necessity of SOLIDARITY and CREDIBILITY 25

Destined to BE … 32

Raising Children beyond the Color Line 36

Live in fear, or live in engagement? 37

Developing Racial Identity 40

Lasting Impact 43

The Least of These…? 46

White Privilege: A Journey of Initiation and Awareness 50

I know IT is there... 59

Siento Enojado (I Feel Angry) 64

MAKING PEACE WITH MESTIZO 66

Black Robes And Pomp, In A World Of Despair 75

Sangre por Sangre 79

Drivin' today from my 'hood to the other 85

Real Peace: What Will it Take? 86

Street-wize Eyez 91

DAKOTA JOURNEY 94

On the Road to Crow Creek 98

Sunset Over Crow Creek 100

As Day Comes to a Close Over the SD Plains: New Insights and Friendships Emerge 102

Sunset Over Woonsocket SD 107

Riding to Howard SD, Following the Ancient Dakota Highway. 110

Letter emailed 112

Riding Together to Live Together 116

Standing in Solidarity with the Dakota this December 26 119

Dakota 38+2 Memorial Ride Nears Mankato 122

Silent Night, Holy Night; the Gallows are Ready for Brothers in Christ 124

Bleached of the Struggle 127

Postlogue 129

Forward

"These writings bring an authenticity and transparency that is needed if reconciliation is going to continue to impact lives in urban centers and beyond. The mixture of faith, life experience, and poetry lifts up the historic connection between art, religion, and justice."

Efrem Smith, Founding Pastor of the Sanctuary Evangelical Covenant Church and Author of "Raising Up Young Heroes," "Jump: Going Further and Higher" and "The Post Black & Post White Church." Currently he is the President and CEO of World Impact

"Marque Jensen has played an instrumental part of the worship experience at the Sanctuary Covenant Church; he is someone I value as a colleague and as a friend. His passion as an agent of change spills over upon every person he meets.

I've enjoyed reading these poems and stories. Marque has shared some of them as spoken words during our worship experiences. They are a glimpse into of his personal journey and quest to discover God's truth. I've enjoyed being part of and a witness to this journey.

May this book change your life and the life of every person who comes in contact with these true stories and heartfelt thoughts."

Sherrie Jones
Worship Experience Director
Sanctuary Covenant Church

To the reader

As you read through these stories, my hope is that you will leave asking more questions rather than feeling as if you have all the answers. These are personal reflections, not theological statements, however I pray they will help you glimpse the heart of the Almighty.

A couple of things to consider as you read:

You will note this is not your traditional niche book. I hope people of all faiths may explore and discuss the topics included; I seek to live and write in a way that is inclusive to all. Yet because of my background and history, I know it has direct application to the Christian community.

A result of the journey I have been on is that I have grown tired of legalistic Christianity. You know the kind that is more obsessed with looking "good" than with resembling Jesus. Instead, I am drawn to the man who was called a drunkard and a glutton just because of the friends he kept.

I believe this book can be a helpful discussion starter and a guide for people of all racial and cultural backgrounds. True, white Americans typically lag behind people of color in their ability to see, understand, and discuss the complex realities of race and culture, and so this book is designed to help them begin and continue on that journey.

Yet, while people of color are typically more racially and culturally aware, it does *not* automatically mean they are better equipped to help navigate and build Beloved Community. This is a result of generations of oppression that has been administered in varying degrees, depending on one's social and economic standing. Because of this painful legacy, one's racial awareness may be rooted bitterness or exclusiveness, and not a hopeful vision inclusive of all. Unless understood and addressed, such attitudes will work to diminish, not build the beloved community.

Ojala, (I sincerely hope/pray that) these short stories and poems when digested in the midst of a diverse community can serve to nourish and energize *all* in the journey to create communities that are inclusive, just and loving.

First remember, this is a cross-cultural dialogue, thanks to the words and thoughts of my friends who are embedded in these pages. As a real multi-cultural conversation there will be things uncomfortable and unclear. I've left in slang, some explicit language, and I didn't translate all the Spanish. These stories are from the real world where things are messy, not always filtered and sanitized, and at times needing some clarification. If you need some help, use the "urban dictionary" or Google, or just call a friend; you may start your own conversation.

Secondly, I hope these stories prompt discussions. The questions after each section are designed to stimulate, not limit discussion and thought. I did not place questions after the poetry, however as I wanted each person / group to interact with those words in ways that resonated personally.

I never want to portray myself as THE example of how to "do" urban, multi-cultural life. This is the journey I've taken and this is NOT the path the Creator may want others to follow. BUT, I do hope in conversations with people of other races and cultures you will find the path that is best for you.

Acknowledgements

I know the stories leave out TONS of people and experiences. Sorry to all not named. But I do want to add a short list of persons to thank *in addition to those in the book*:

Early on Professor, Dr. Paul Macalister challenged me to think big and trust God with my life, as well as many other amazing professors and mentors; Cachiaras, Grice, Friddel, and Picker, from **Minnesota Bible College**, now Crossroads College.

I wish I could mention by name all the great people who were a part of **North Minneapolis Christian Fellowship**. Our co-workers and staff have been a HUGE part of my journey. In addition to Nate and Sherri Orr are: Elwood and Betty, Jackie, Tim and Jennifer, Stacey and Tryeneyse, Brad and Jean, Tom and Barb, Bonnie, Joel and Lori, as well as Linda and Margaret.

The great people at **Sanctuary Covenant Church and Community Development Corp.** who help encourage and inspire me: Pastors Efrem, Cecilia, Kevin, and Sandy, also Chris, Sherri, Jeremy, J-Mo, Iomos, Neeraj, Jen, Heidi, Carl, Jamel, and Paul.

I am grateful to my **Dakota / Lakota brothers** who have been welcoming and patient helping me begin to understand and appreciate the beauty of their culture and shown me the meaning of "Mitakuye Oyasin."

Thanks Jim Miller and Alberta Iron Cloud, Peter Lengkeek, Richard Milda, Jim Bear Jacobs, Jake, Seth, Guy and all the young brothers and sisters / prayer warriors, I can't begin to name you all, but you know who you are; I'm proud to call you my friends.

I have to mention mi jefe y compañero, Jose (Ivan) with **Minne-Mex Construction**. Since our chance meeting he has become a good friend, brother and co-worker and boss. Also gracias a Armando, la familia Martínez', (de Monterrey y de Minnesota) y a todos de la raza que me reciben como un hermano.

Besides all those who read and gave suggestions, Ariah Fine, Jessica Mueller, Matthew Spillum, and Jared Cox really helped with editing. Cody Buck - thanks for getting me writing more of the stories to pass along! Jeremy Scheller, "you the man!" for the sweet cover art.

Finally to my **wife Janeen**, who has encouraged and stood by me in this crazy journey, along with our **children Jared, Tyler and Morgan**. Thanks too, to the special people in their lives, **Angela, Phoebe, and Josh,** who have contributed with your feedback and ideas.

Thanks, and I love you all so much!

INTRODUCTION

Ever since my college years, going for a run has been my quiet time. I guess it make sense for someone that has been unofficially diagnosed as having ADHD that quiet cannot be motionless. I've learned how to cope with me. When I jog, the world becomes still and clear and I am able to better commune with the Creator.

While on a recent run, I began to think about all the lessons God has taught me here in North Minneapolis, even lessons I've learned while on a run. For example: After scaring a few people, and almost getting slugged once or twice, I have learned not to run up on people without giving some warning. I've also learned the power of friendliness and confidence in discovering how a look and nod can earn respect, and dispel the prejudice and fear that stereotypes perpetrate.

On this run, I was also vividly aware of the over twenty years of interaction with these streets, homes, and intersections ...this is the corner where that kid got shot one hot fall day ...this is the house where Jamil, Eric and I used to hang out on the front steps with all the boys on the block ... this the corner where my sons showed they knew how to drop and crawl when gun-play got too close ... and this is the wading pool where all three of my kids spent many hot days cooling down with friends.

Lessons and memories; mostly good, some bad, yet God was and is at work through them all. I write these stories, not because my wife, Janeen, and I are some great role models, but because we believe they are a demonstration of God's grace and provision. In this journey God has taught us much through the people with whom we have journeyed.

Full Circle, Under a Full Moon, on a Sledding Hill

Tonight I went to one of my favorite spots in Minneapolis: Theodore Wirth Sledding Hill. In the summer, it's just a boring golf course that seems to be off-limits to me and most of my friends (*To be fair, I hear it is a nice course, but I've never made it past a few forays on the par-3*). But on a winter night, it becomes an enchanted playground. The crowds that create a cacophony of voices and yells in the daytime slowly slip away as shadows lengthen with the setting sun. The Minneapolis skyline shimmers in the east, appearing just out of reach, but you are surrounded on all other sides by wooded hills. If you have the good fortune of being there under a full moon, the enchantment is magnified.

We have been coming here for years. We sometimes join in with the daytime crowds, but my favorite times are at night, usually after 10 or 11pm. This is a place for youth groups, school friends, birthday parties and more. Going to "Theo-Wirth" has become a family ritual, and I'm glad to say my children continue to go, bring their friends, and keep the tradition.

So last night, as we were sledding and eating the wings we were grilling at the top of the hill, I shared with the guys about the farm where I grew up. It was over 30 years ago, and seems like another, almost fictional, life, yet many of the memories are so fresh that the smells still linger.

Our dairy farm was situated at the base of a good-sized hill (for Iowa). It wasn't huge, but it impacted day-to-day life. It shielded the house and barn from harsh winds, and if the starter went out on a tractor, you parked it on the hill to roll-start it. When there was snow or ice *you* had to adjust; the hill did not move.

On this hill, my love for sledding and winter nights was birthed. The main barn was built into the hill, and the dairy and house were below. Up on the hill were the huts and pens for the calves that needed daily personal hand feeding with the morning and evening chores. That meant trudging up and down the hill multiple times, hauling milk and feed in 5 gallon buckets. Friends say that's how my calves (on my legs, not the baby cows) got so big.

The hill took on a different feel in the winter. On every trip I made up the hill, I would pull along a sled. Sometimes I would pull the grain on the sled, and then my return trip could become a short vacation. Frequently, I would need to bring a bale of hay down the hill, and that, too, fit nicely on my sled. I would lie across it for the exciting and occasionally treacherous ride to the bottom; over ice, dodging parked vehicles, pets, and buildings.

Farm life on a dairy, is all about work, family, and working together. Even if I were up and working at 5 or 6 am, my dad would remind me that I'd already missed the best part of the day. The cows needed their date with the milking machine, calves needed feeding, and the day didn't end until all the bovine were content.

Summer added another layer of activity: field work. On our family farm, we raised corn, hay, and soybeans primarily to feed the animals all year long. Now, besides getting an early start for chores, one also had to get the hay stored away in the barns, and crops planted, cultivated and harvested. It was hard work, but I always looked forward to long hours in the dairy barn or on the tractor with an FM radio as my only compadre.

It was here I fell in love with music; in addition to the hymns we sang at church, my family had introduced me to the Statler Brothers, and my small town loved John Denver. However, alone on the tractor and with the cows, the top 40 hits I loved the most were the likes of KC and the Sunshine Band, Peaches & Herb, The O'Jays and Sister Sledge. I loved funk and disco even though I knew nothing of its origin or practice; I just liked how it sounded. This was the late 70's before Internet, before downloads. I rarely visited record stores and never got to watch American Bandstand (Saturday morning was for work!), so it was only in later years that I learned much of the music that pulsed in my soul was created by African Americans.

I can't help but wonder if these musical seeds were being planted to prepare me for my future. For it was during this time in the Bronx of New York that social injustice and musical fusion united with technological innovation and community inspiration to conceive Hip-Hop. Within the next few years, I would be exposed to this new expression of motion and rhythms. My heart was being prepared for what my mind would need to comprehend.

My years on the farm laid other foundations for my future urbanization. At that time, our farm was one of the largest and most modernized in that part of Iowa. We frequently had visitors from around the world who were studying at Iowan universities. My parents welcomed these visitors from Asian and African countries, from Mexico, the Caribbean and the rest of Latin America.

In the 60's and 70's, "ethnic foods" like pizza and tacos had just made their debut in northeast Iowa. I had yet to try stir-fried rice, Szechwan or Jerk chicken, but as a child I was being blessed to meet people, not just flavors, from other lands. More importantly, my parents taught us to see our guests not as peculiar, but as familiar. My country experiences were in these ways quite unique from many of my peers. True, I was still sheltered and unaware of most of the racial and cultural realities of our time, however, my upbringing gave me a framework of cross-cultural experiences upon which to build.

I was quite ignorant and even prejudiced about the city. For all the positive messages I was given regarding people of various races and cultures, I was trained to be suspicious of and fear the city and those who dwelt there. It was no secret to us in the country; God created man and woman in the garden, or you could say "on the farm." Truth is, mankind only built cities after the fall. Coincidence? Not from the perspective of the prairie theologian.

As a family, we made few trips to the city. Why anyone would want to live there was beyond our imagination. On a family vacation we once ventured into Seattle, then on through Los Angeles and on to Pomona. We went out of curiosity and obligation to visit family members who were either "unfortunate" or "foolish" enough to live there. On another trip, I was a fascinated 13-year-old, watching wide-eyed as we took the wrong exit to the Gateway Arch, and instead wound up in East St. Louis. "Kids, lock your doors!" Mom firmly gave us the same safety instructions as she frequently did when we were in East Waterloo on our way to visit the only major hospital in the area. I wasn't sure why she said that, but I knew the only similarity between St. Louis and Waterloo, besides being the EAST part of the city, was the darker complexion of the residents.

With this perspective, I made my first trip into Minneapolis at the malleable age of eighteen. I remember traveling up I-35. Once we were in the city, I marveled at the high walls they had built along the freeway. Over the years I had helped build miles of fence to keep out cows, but these walls were designed to keep everything out. Were those walls there to protect those in their cars from the dangers that lurked behind those walls? I wasn't sure, but as we drove through Minneapolis and past the newly built Metrodome, I was thanking God that I did not live in such a place. We crossed the Mississippi River and safely made it to the Amtrak station in St. Paul. I was curious about the city, but vowed I would never make it my home.

On the day I moved to college, I got up extra early. After finishing my chores I grabbed my favorite graduation present, a Pentax K1000, my 35mm camera. I headed out to the woods that lined the creek that ran about 1/2 mile from our home. We pastured out cattle in these wooded hills. I knew the area well, every bend of the stream, hill and ravine. I had searched for newborn calves among these trees and bushes. This was my home, where we worked, camped, and played.

I was often aware that less than 130 years prior to my treks, there were other young men who played and lived here: the First Americans. There was an ignorant innocence, and yet a strangely clear awareness that this land had many more stories to tell. I understood in my heart that even though my father owned this land, the land had a life of its own.

I spent up most of a 36 exposure roll of film that morning. I clicked pictures of flowers, downed logs with moss, and birds. I got shots of the creek running over slick rocks. I was confident I would be back and spend the remainder of my life on that farm. It was not to be.

In some strange way, I was aware that the world as I knew it, was about to drastically change. I have returned to wander those woods many times since. However, the maxim, "You can never return home again," seems to have held true. The trees and hills remain much the same, but my life was to be molded over the next 30 years in ways beyond my comprehension.

I love my city, yet I still love being in woods and, as surprising as it is to my city friends, I am still a natural on the farm. That other maxim, "You can take the boy off the farm, but you can't take the farm out of the boy," is also true. While something deep within me has been altered, I've also discovered farm and urban culture share many similarities.

My life was turned upside-down and sideways. NOT because of what I brought to the city, but because of what the city and her people brought to me. A mosaic of people added their colors and spices to the content of my being, soul, my very "SER."

The people of the city have given themselves to me, in turn, they have made me multi-cultural. So here I am. At home in North Minneapolis, yet not 100% native to this community; but then who is? I can't go back, and even if I would physically, I would feel out of place emotionally and socially.

In my own journey of identity, I realize none of us really belong, we just seek to fit and fulfill our calling. Identity is a quest we can never really fulfill on our own. Personal identity is, in part, a function of community as we allow others to fill in the missing pieces of our mosaic with their own colors.

This sledding hill in the city is a metaphor of my identity: an urban boy with country roots who loves sledding, Hip-Hop, and adventures with friends. The place we are born sets the stage for the first act of our life, but birth does not define the script and settings of the conclusion. It is the community that encircles us, challenges and inspires us, that helps craft our narrative. These are stories of people, places, and ideas that have flavored my salsa, highlighted my tapestry, and impacted the very trajectory of my life.

Consider...

Were there any stories, examples from Marque's life that you could relate to?

Looking back on your childhood, what are some experiences that unexpectedly shaped your future?

How does (and has) your community/environment influence your identity?

Are there places about which you have said, "I could never live there..." if so why?

Have you had experiences with food, culture, and/or people that changed your perspectives?

The Human Race

We've struggled for years to find equality

That human place of co-existence and friendship.

We feel it better than describe it.

It seems to deny us, allude us, and lead us astray.

Perhaps we are looking in the wrong place.

A star-lit, cold Minnesota night,

Is the place I find right,

Boots crunch in the snow,

Sleds soar, voices roar.

But silence and cold rule

Allowing young and old of every pigmentation

Equal opportunity to be free in the frozen.

Side by side dressed in bulk and layers

We are one race.

We race for fun, for the challenge.

There is more that unites than divides.

We must race to survive!

A Journey to Solidarity and Credibility

I recently had the opportunity to meet Dr. Soong-Chan Rah, of North Park Seminary in Chicago. Prior to his present position as a professor, he was pastor of a multi-racial church in the Boston area. As a Korean American, Soong-Chan has a wonderfully unique, yet thoroughly biblical, view of Christianity. He also frustrates and offends many defenders of traditional westernized Christianity.

In "The Next Evangelicalism: Freeing the Church from Western Cultural Captivity," he explores how the face of evangelicalism is changing as non-whites become not only the majority, but the driving force of the evangelical church. I have heard him frequently make the comment that "…if you are a European-American Christian desiring to minister among another culture and race, yet have never been taught or mentored by anyone other than from your own racial/cultural group, you most likely will not be doing evangelism, you will primarily be doing the work of a colonizer." Wow! Is he saying that all those good intentioned white folks going forth to save the colored heathen may be doing more harm than good?

I came to North Minneapolis having never heard this; it wasn't a concern to the white professors and pastors who had taught me. While they were aware of the need to culturally contextualize the Good News, it was always assumed that the normative starting point of understanding scripture was through the lenses of Western European and American traditions. However, long before Dr. Rah taught this, God understood it.

This is why God used Moses, trained by Egyptians, to lead the Israelites from Egypt. This is why God used Saul, who was trained by not only Hebrews, but also by Romans and Greeks, to bring the Good News to the Gentiles. The same Lord has allowed me to learn from relationships filled with laughter, anger, tears, and love that His image is imprinted on all people from every culture and race.

The Gift of PERSPECTIVE across Culture

God first began to teach me this lesson as a child on the farm in Iowa. As I mentioned earlier, my parents believed the simple gospel message that "God so loved the world." They understood that their creator equally valued all peoples and nations. My dad demonstrated this several times to the occasional "black" or "brown" family that would show-up in our all-white community. He would reach out with help, encouragement and even words of defense to accusing and racist neighbors. I learned at a young age that certain words and attitudes were not Godly and would not be tolerated in my home. This was something I never remember being told, it was simply demonstrated.

My father tells the story of how one time in the late 60's, a white neighbor (which is a redundancy) drove to our farm and jumped out of his truck to exclaim, "Pete, did you know there are n***ers hunting on your land?" My dad just looked at him and replied, "well, that makes 'em better men than you, 'cuz they asked." The neighbor muttered something and drove off.

Only in recent years have I really appreciated this courage. True, it may seem a small thing, however it was a gutsy act in the late '60s. Few white men would dare call a black man "better" than a fellow white. In recent years, I learned that my great aunt took my father on trips to see America in the 1940's when he was a pre-teen. One of the places she took him was the segregated South. She was an English professor from upper New York who wanted to observe it first hand; she also wanted to expose her nephew to the strange and troubled world of legally mandated segregation.

My dad recalls his aunt telling him he could not use the 'colored' toilets, yet had not prohibited him from trying out the 'colored' drinking fountains. He laughs about how he snuck over to one to see what color the water would be, and was disappointed when it looked like regular water. Years later, while a young GI stationed in Korea and Japan, he served in some of the first integrated army units. He has shared that those relationships, while not deep, had an impact on his perspectives. All these experiences enlightened the way my father thought and talked about people of various races.

I am also thankful that my small country church was obliged to teach me at a young age that "...we really don't know what Jesus looked like, but we do know he wasn't white." I was just a kid of six or seven years when a young man from our church returned home from the Vietnam War. He came back to Iowa with his family, married to a Vietnamese woman. Their two children became part of my Sunday School class.

This man gave a special gift to our church: a painting of Jesus. It was unlike any we had ever seen. It was a "Vietnamese" Jesus. It was clearly a Jesus painting. I mean, you know one when you see it. Yet, having been painted by a Christian in Vietnam, Jesus had facial shape, hair, and eyes with a distinctly Vietnamese look. I vaguely remember some conflict around the picture within the church. I recall hearing my parents say, "We don't know what Jesus looked like... we do know he was Jewish and he wasn't white, but that doesn't matter, He was for all of us..." I still had a lot to learn, but my parents' perspective made some of my future transitions much easier to navigate.

I went to a small Christian College in Rochester, Minnesota. At the time it was Minnesota Bible College (MBC), now it is Crossroads College. All my professors and most of my classmates were white. In spite of being culturally isolated, they did a fairly good job of exposing us to differing perspectives and challenging us with a mindset to "missions" that was unique for the time. We heard from guest preachers and lecturers who were from India, Latin America, and others who challenged our perspectives.

The professors who taught evangelism and missions challenged us to understand that the gospel must be holistic, not just about saving souls, and it must be contextualized, meeting people in the context of their culture. It was here that I began to see that Christian ministry cannot be about me imposing my views and beliefs without taking into account another's culture and experiences. While it took years for this concept to become more clearly focused, I am thankful I was given a lens with which I could begin to see people and scripture from a different perspective.

Consider...

What comments/attitudes about race and cultures do you remember hearing from family and friends as a child?

How did this impact your perspectives?

Do you know what prior experiences had shaped your family/friends attitudes?

Does this community continue to impact your views?

The Call to RISK beyond Race and Class

One guest preacher who deeply influenced my life was James Lane. James was, and still is, the pastor at North End Christian Church in Hartford, CT. He came to our small college for "Spiritual Emphasis Week," an annual mid-winter conference. I think it was designed to keep us from getting a serious case of cabin fever. Anyway, they always brought in a special guest speaker to the regular chapel services. In the evenings, there were meals and discussions as well.

I don't remember anything specific Pastor Lane preached or taught, but I do recall being challenged to consider the "crisis" in urban America. My eyes were being opened to the reality of race and class and the importance of the American Church in addressing the resulting disparities. I'm quite sure he was the first African-American I had ever heard preach. I met with him several times during his visit to our school. We exchanged information and stayed in contact.

The next year, I married Janeen and we were trying to discern what direction to go in our lives. We thought a trip to volunteer and serve in various places would help us see the next steps more clearly. Originally, we planned a trip to India where I would have the opportunity to work with a campus ministry while getting my Masters Degree in Chennai. However the assassination of Indira Ghandi closed the country to Americans and forced a change to our plans. We connected with people we knew in Scotland and also called Pastor James in Hartford. As a result, we crafted a unique experience; a fortnight in Tunbridge Wells, a small city in southern England; a month on the North Sea in Buckie, Scotland; a week traveling; two more weeks in inner-city London, and then our last two and half weeks with Pastor Lane in Hartford and New York City.

The experience had a profound impact. This adventure demonstrated to us that wherever we were, we could be at peace, because God was already there and so were people. If God's people were there, we quickly discovered we had family as well.

In the church in London (a contact James made for us), we had our first experience of living with people of African-ancestry. It was a Jamaican-British family. In our short time there, we learned about sugar on popcorn, "Eastenders," and racism. We didn't realize it at the time, but looking back, it appears we stayed in "the projects." One day, the community awoke to see that a white-power group had painted racist slogans on the front side of the apartment complex. Later that week, the son returned from school talking about how he had been racially harassed in the school. That lens I had been given in college was being polished; I struggled to see how their experiences interfaced with the Christianity I had experienced in Iowa. They worshiped the same Christ, yet seemed to encounter him so differently.

After leaving England, we returned to the USA and went to Hartford. I mused that although I was in *my native country*, nothing in North Hartford seemed like *my culture*. Pastor James challenged us to get out and see the neighborhood. Heeding his advice, we quickly familiarized ourselves with the community. I would go jogging, Janeen and I walked to the corner store, we went to people's homes for meals and helped at a shelter where Pastor Lane worked.

Yet, I struggled to understand what people were saying, I got angry at the homeless men who didn't appreciate my service, and I was confused when people thought it was stupid for me to walk around the neighborhood snapping pictures with my big Pentax K1000. I was an ignorant white boy, fresh from the Midwest, but James saw potential he wanted to challenge.

As we drove to New York, where we would spend our last four days in Spanish Harlem, James told me two things I've never forgotten. First, he told me that effectiveness does not depend on the *culture you come from*, but the *heart you bring*. Similar to that unforgettable Rakim line, "It's not where you from, it's where you at!"

He explained to me how he observes that people are often more likely to listen and learn from someone different from them than like them, "... Think about Jesus, his hometown people didn't hear him, because they thought they knew him. That's how it is for me. If I go to an all black community often they are like, "oh... yawn ... we've heard this before," and they turn me off. But if I go to a little farm town in the mid-west, people will be like... "Wow, I should listen to this. This guy has something different to say, yet I can tell he really cares. Why else would he have come here?" People in the city, black, Latino, white, really might listen to you better than me because they realize you came because you *wanted* to, not because you *had to*.

Secondly, James gave me this challenge: "Think about a knife. Most of the knife is made up of the handle and the broad part of the blade. Without those parts the cutting edge would not be able to do anything. The handle and the thick part of the blade provide the support, yet the part of the knife that does the real work is in the few molecules along that cutting edge. Where do you want to be? Where do you want to live your life, In the security of the handle or the backside of the blade? Or... on the cutting edge?"

James opened my eyes to how the Church had forgotten and forsaken the city, especially low income persons of color. My lens was being focused even more.

We've never returned to Hartford, but James' words and challenge help set the trajectory of our lives. James came to visit us shortly after we moved to Minneapolis. We shared with him how many of our friends and family were appalled that we had moved into "the 'hood." He looked at us, smiled and said, "You ain't got bars on your windows and you got grass on your lawns... this aint the hood!" He helped us see we could take what we had been given and use it wherever we might be. Without his challenges and encouragement, we may have never been ready for the relationships and experiences God was about to bring to us in Minneapolis.

Consider...

Has your "lens" for viewing scripture, culture and people changed over your life? How? Why?

What do you think about James' comment about culture and heart?

In what types of situations do you think "heart" alone can cross the cultural gap? It what situations would you say it can't?

What are the advantages of your cultural perspectives? What are the disadvantages?

What are the advantages and disadvantages of living in the "handle" or on the blade? Where do you typically see yourself?

The Beauty of a COMMUNITY filled with Diversity

We landed in Minneapolis at a place called Southeast Christian Church. It was near downtown and next to the University of Minnesota. The church had made an agreement with the park across the street to share a youth worker. I was to work with the youth in the church and in the neighborhood. It was primarily a "University" church, with many college-educated urbanites who had come to the church during their schooling, and stuck around. However our youth group quickly became a much more diverse crew and because of this, it was a great place for my "urban initiation."

We started with the kids whose parents went to the church, then reached out to their friends and other kids in the neighborhood. It was 1987; I knew nothing about Christian Community Development, Institutional Racism, White Privilege, Reconciliation or Relocation. There were few (if any) colleges with classes, much less degrees, in "Urban Studies." However, this group of high school youth became my educators in urban life. Almost everywhere we went, we brought diversity to the environmental pudding. In many places, like the camp I had been part of for years, we brought the rich chocolate. In other contexts, we brought the vanilla, as well as some salsa. These kids and their families baptized us in the joy of diversity in Christ, a confidence in the city, and taste of community that would help chart the course for our future.

Also at this time, there were many who introduced me to academic and social concepts that would give me the language and intellectual tools needed to process these experiences. I was blessed to meet and learn from many, including Art Erickson, Curtiss DeYoung, Karen McKinney, Nicholas Cooper-Lewter, and others through the emerging "Twin Cities Urban Network" (TURN) as well as through informal gatherings. A friend gave me *Urban Christian* by Ray Bakke. I'm usually a slow reader, but I tore through it in just a few days. I couldn't believe there were people who understood what I was experiencing, and I soaked up each opportunity I had to learn and grow.

The students in our youth group were scattered from one end of Minneapolis to the other. I had students in four different high schools and I quickly saw the economic and racial disparities of the city first hand. I was naively convinced that if other Christians just saw what I saw and knew what I knew, they all would quickly sign-up to become part of the solution.

My first sustained venture in North Minneapolis came as a result of a summer program I began through Crossroads College. "God's Hands" was designed to give rural and suburban youth both awareness and experience with urban America. We would spend a week at the college campus in Rochester, then come to Minneapolis where we worked in shelters, with youth programs, churches, and in street evangelism. One of our partner organizations was Hospitality House. Nathaniel Orr, who had worked at Hospitality House for years, was one of our key contacts and trainers each summer.

An Awareness of INCOMPLETENESS

When I first met Nate, my views about race and culture were very simple.

I, like most good-white-Christians of the 80's said we believed in the vision of Dr. Martin Luther King Jr.; a world where we would be judged by the "… content of our character, not on the color of our skin." I knew some about slavery, a little about civil rights, and I realized racism was real and powerful. But I had no idea how it had forced whites and blacks to develop such very different cultures. I had no idea how deeply distrust and suspicions were rooted. I was to learn that distrust and suspicion were not just in the hearts of white folks like me, but also in the hearts of well-intentioned people like Nathaniel.

I believe "passion without wisdom" is one of the greatest barriers of moving into racial reconciliation. Many share the wish of Rodney King, "… can we all get along?" But they don't want to take the time to learn about the historical baggage that has been strapped to all of our backs, nor do they want to listen to the struggle of others in dealing with that baggage. Most of us begin with the assumption that what *I* have observed and experienced is normative for all. With that ignorance we are destined to quickly offend.

Nate and I soon realized that if we moved past the I, we could help unpack each other's bags. We would also learn that as we moved beyond the socially acceptable racial roles ascribed to us in America, we both would face alienation from some of our acquaintances. I was unaware of how hard it would be to forge a real, mutual, friendship across culture and race. I was also unaware of how much of a gift and blessing our relationship would become.

Within two years from first meeting Nathaniel, I had moved with my wife and year old son to North Minneapolis. We found our house while I was student teaching at North High School. Even though I was still the youth pastor at Southeast Christian Church, I began to partner more with Hospitality House. It provided a tangible means for connection with our neighbors and my students in the high school. During this time my relationship with Nate continued to grow.

In addition to involvement with Hospitality House we had also hosted "Backyard Bible Clubs," I had volunteered as a tutor and coach at the park, and we had been involved in other events with our neighbors. One early fall day I was walking to the bus to go to work at our church across the river. One of the neighbor girls ran up to me and began bombarding me with questions. Eventually she blurted out, "When are we gonna have another kids club?" I remember thinking, "Girl, it's fall! We ain't doing that again till next summer."

I was shocked at both my callousness and at her openness. I mumbled something to the effect that we'd see what we could do, but made no promises. As I rode across town, I wondered what the future held; I felt like I was being undone and yet redone. I knew our time at the church across the river was coming to a close, and our commitment to this community was about to intensify.

Southeast Christian Church had been an exceptional place for my family and me. It was also a welcoming community for our new neighbors in North Minneapolis. We frequently brought people with us to their services and youth programs, but there was always something "difficult" in taking our neighbors out of their neighborhood. The problem was we were taking people to *other* programs. It was time for us to have something that would be *ours*. God was about to open a new chapter in our life and in our community.

Shortly after my conversation with that neighbor girl, Nathaniel and I were standing out front of the Hospitality House talking. I told him I was considering starting a church in our neighborhood and would love to have him as a partner. After a period of considering the opportunity in prayer and discussing it with his wife, he came back to me with a solid and confident, YES! Little did either of us know the impact that decision would have on every area of our lives.

Consider…

The last 3 sections were about RISK, BEAUTY, and AWARENESS -

How have you taken risks to cross racial and cultural divides?

What were the results?

Do you see your own perspectives and culture as incomplete? Why or why not?

If so, how did this awareness develop?

What are examples of the "beauty" of diversity you have experienced?

How have you seen "passion without wisdom" displayed? What have been the results?

The Cost of RELATIONSHIPS that reflect Heaven

Early on in planting the new church, Nate and I realized that for the church to succeed our relationship needed to thrive. We began to speak of our venture as not just a partnership, but as a covenant, similar to a marriage that both of us were sworn to uphold. I had never been engaged in such a stimulating and yet frustrating relationship. Time and again, after hanging up from a long conversation with Nate, my wife would timidly ask, " …is everything ok?" She wondered, from hearing half of the conversation, if we had had been fighting. I often left these conversations confused. Why did things that I thought were simple and straightforward demand so much discussion? I didn't know what issues were racial, and which were Nate-and-Marque issues. At times I wondered if it was worth it. The novelties and niceties of a unique relationship quickly wore off, yet I found a sense of deep satisfaction as well.

We were committed to each other, our families, and our community. We recited the mantra, "… as goes our relationship, so goes the church." We knew that if we were to see a church on this earth that reflected the image of heaven (where persons of every language and ethnicity gathered in unity to worship and serve the Lord) we had to learn how to live out our relationship in reconciled unity. We understood that "Tolerance" was not an option, simply "respecting diversity" would soon get old, but real reconciliation required a new level of sacrifice and transformation.

One of the most damaging residues of racism is that it allows us to think of others in less than fully human terms. Racism undercuts relationship-building. It programs us so that we think of others primarily in terms of race-based prejudices. This in turn allow us to dismiss their experiences and narratives. I understood that I had to deal with my own prejudices, but one night, sitting by our garage talking, I was struck by a new thought: Not only do I have racial prejudices to unravel, but Pastor Nathaniel has racial lenses that color how he sees and hears me."

Our racially tinted vision confronted us early on our journey. I had made a decision regarding church bookkeeping that I now wanted to reverse. I had asked Nate to manage the books and write the checks. My initial decision was made in good faith, but on later evaluation, it didn't seem to match with Nathaniel's gifts, and another person was now willing to assume part of the responsibility. However to Nate, there was a strong suspicion that my decision had nothing to do with ability and gifts, but it was another example of how "white folks don't trust black folks with money." This was one of those moments where we had to own the fact that we both had come with baggage, much of it unneeded, and we could either carry it alone or let the other help unpack it.

We understood that our relationship had to serve as a model to all others in the church. While this sounds simple and straightforward, it was anything but. In the middle of our first all-church retreat, my wife was crying and Nate's wife, Sherri, was frustrated. Sherri had just raised the point that the pastors' children would be an example to other parents as to how we expect children to behave in the church service. This is when my young, Scandinavian-American bride started to get uncomfortable.

Nate and Sherri had two girls that knew how to sit and listen, we had two hyperactive boys that wanted to run and talk. The Orrs came from a cultural tradition where the village helps to raise each child, and will scold when needed. Additionally, in African-American tradition difficult issues are discussed and confronted openly. Janeen and I came from a cultural tradition where no one helps to raise, much less scold, another's child. In Scandinavian/Germanic-American culture, difficult issues are usually pushed aside and only confronted when you are at your wit's end. In the tradition of Janeen and my families, churches would rather split than openly deal with an issue.

And so at this retreat, I was extremely uncomfortable; on the one side, my co-pastor's wife was making a culturally and socially appropriate request. On the other side was my wife, the mother of my boys, who was getting defensive and feeling shamed. That was the beginning of a long journey for Janeen and Sherri, a journey that has caused them both to shed tears, shape attitudes, and emerge personally transformed. They have physically and culturally taken each other to places they would not have gone alone.

Today, Sherri and Janeen are friends who will call each other at time of need or just to share a good shopping bargain. Like real sisters, they are women who will defend each other and confront each other when needed. All of our children have benefited by their parents' unique relationships.

Reconciliation is a strange beast; if you let it in one area of your life, it will soon begin to demand its way into others. The relationship we were forging would go on to challenge and restructure the way we dealt with our spouses, children, and friends. As we journeyed down the path of racial-reconciliation, we were forced to reconsider what honesty, respect, and solidarity looked like in most every area of our lives.

Nate taught me that dishonesty is not just in what I tell him, it is also in what I refuse to tell him. I clearly recall Nate telling me, "you haven't been truthful…" and, I would think, "…but I've not said anything untrue." He would reply, "… you had a problem with this or that and you didn't tell me, you let me think everything was ok, when it wasn't, and THAT is dishonesty." This understanding has cajoled me from my passive-aggressive, mid-western whiteness into the person I am today.

Eventually, we learned to expect, and even play into, the ingrained prejudices of the people around us. For example, people would come into the church needing money and they would always go for the white guy. Why? They believed that white folks in the 'hood are usually bleeding hearts and suckers, wanting to do good and relieve their guilt, but not discerning. So the white pastor was easy game. However, they would assume that the black pastor was from the community, street-wise, and would see right through your game if you were lying.

Nate pointed this out to me. At first I insisted this wasn't happening, but eventually he convinced me and I began to see it with my own eyes. So we decided that all benevolence requests would be processed through him. As a result, people learned that the black man was compassionate and the white man wasn't a sucker. Nate, with the help of others, has shown me the difference between patronizing the poor and being willing to partner and walk with them. Now, some may think "partnering" is a blanket approval of negative behavior. It is not. However, it does create a place where sincere and constructive conversation can take place.

Frequently, Nate and I would subtly (and other times not so subtly) confront prejudice. As we'd visit churches in the suburbs, Nate pointed out to me how white leaders would ask me all significant questions and rarely even look at him. Again, I was initially blind to this phenomenon, but once aware, I committed myself to action. If I observed this happening, I would do my best to push the unsuspecting person out of their comfort zone and into direct conversation with Nate. These types of behaviors often made the "immediate" more difficult, but our commitment to a process of mutual reconciliation made it sustainable.

In these and so many other ways, Janeen and I have been given the gift of heaven prematurely; a community of diverse persons worshiping and living united. We have been able to enjoy many perspectives, traditions, and a fuller picture of humanity and of God. My wife and I both agree; we could never go back to a monocultural existence. We've tasted this aspect of heaven, and we ain't goin' back.

The Necessity of SOLIDARITY and CREDIBILITY

Any time we move into a significant relationship, it will impact who we are and how we view the world. After just a few months of living in North Minneapolis, I began to sense awkwardness in situations that used to feel normal. Things as simple as a comment from a bunch of college friends, a joke at church, or political/racial comments at a family meal; statements and attitudes I would have not thought twice about just a year or two before, now passed through a filter of perspective I was developing from my urban brothers and sisters.

In 1 Corinthians 12, the apostle Paul writes about being ONE body in Christ. He makes the point that if we are really united we will rejoice *and* feel pain over the same things. I began to realize one of the costs of my new trans-racial/cultural relationships was a loss of complacency to the joys and struggles of others. If these relationships were *real*, I could NOT be complacent to their feelings and struggles. If Nate is truly my brother, then things that hurt or offend him should, at the very least, have some negative effect on me. This is a key element of being reconciled, of having solidarity.

Solidarity is defined as "...unity or agreement of feeling or action, especially among individuals with a common interest; mutual support within a group." As my circle of brothers and sisters has grown to include Hmong, Mexicans, Dakotas, Lakotas, and more - so has a keen awareness that we are empowered to bear one another's burdens. For this reason, out of the debt of relationships, I feel compelled to utilize any power or position I may have to speak not only thinking of my concerns but of these with whom I share the bond of solidarity. I know my brothers and sisters will do the same for me.

Sherri would always say, "… if we really love each other, we will begin to rub off on each other." She would explain, "I'll begin to like things, even say things, that are from you and you'll pick up on things from me." We see it all the time: how often do we see older couples who finish each other's sentences, and even begin to "look the same." In the same way, when my sister-in-law moved to east Tennessee, it was only a short time until her husband became a fan of the Vols and she began to speak with an Appalachian accent.

Assimilating cultural traits from your environment is normal and expected, with one general exception; in a racialized society, people who absorb cultural traits outside their race may be subject to scorn. Sure, the majority culture usually approves of Blacks, Asians, or Latinos who assimilate into whiteness. This is apparent when white folks say, "I don't even think of you as..." (fill in the blank). Within the urban schools where I've taught, students of color who try to buck the socially ascribed dress and norms of their peers occasionally get ridiculed for "trying to act white." But, while a white Minnesotan can pick up the social habits of white Tennesseans, it is never socially acceptable for white of any state to adopt cultural patterns of blacks (or other racial minorities) in their own community. However, solidarity, real community, will take us places we could never go alone.

I mentioned that Sherri and my wife are shopping buddies. It is more than that, you see, Sherri has the spiritual gift of "community shopper." For a time, in the life of our church, she would show up on most every Sunday morning with one or more bags full of clothing to give to people in the church. It was *always* quality, *often* new, and *never* too expensive. She knew how and where to shop, she knew everyone's size and she loved to love on others by giving gifts.

So it should have been no surprise, when Sherri began to give me clothing that pushed me beyond my racial comfort zones; she began to buy me "urban gear." Now, today that might not seem like a big deal, but this was the early 90's when the delineation between "white" and "black" clothing was seemingly more pronounced. Gifts of friendship are often accompanied by physical gifts. Such was the case with these gifts which over time transformed everything from my wardrobe to my worldview. But this was not merely cultural "posing," "stealing a style for a season" or as some call being a *wigger*. This transformation was gradual and signaled by internal attitudes, awareness and consistency. Consistency will be rewarded with credibility.

Recently, I heard Brenda Salter McNeil talking about cultural competency. She explained that often people feel this is something they can earn on their own. By taking classes, passing tests, we can learn things to help us navigate cultures more fluidly. She went on to explain a concept that she calls "Inter-cultural Credibility." Credibility, she explained, is not something we earn on our own, it is something others bestow on us.

You *earn* credibility. In the 'hood it's called "street cred." I've received many gifts; clothes, food, even bling, but they are all just symbols of what people have really given me: friendship, trust, and solidarity within a community. I had hoped I could become competent, but Sherri and others gave me a gift I could never acquire on my own: credibility.

Years ago, our solidarity with Nate, Sherri, our church community, and the kids and families from our neighborhood, gave us confidence (not without some fear and frustration) to face white Americans angry over Rodney King and O.J. Simpson. They gave us the confidence to stand and speak up for justice in difficult situations. But it must not be forgotten that, for our friends of color, solidarity with us also put them in situations where they stepped up to defend white folks. At times they too suffered a loss of social capital because of their relationships across the social barriers of race.

Being part of a community with this type of mutual support and concern strengthened me to address racist practices lurking in colleges and institutions. I found myself in shared life experiences with young urban students who frequently found themselves overwhelmed at traditional white/suburban colleges. Relationships like these empowered me to see and even feel prejudice and institutional racism.

Some may say that level of solidarity is impossible if you're white. I would never try to say that I can fully understand. I won't pretend to be what I am not. Yet because of sharing space, culture, and views I have several times experienced the kinds of injustice often reserved for people of color. More than once I have been unjustly stopped by police, cuffed and questioned. True solidarity is not only sharing in the food and the slang, but also in the struggle.

One of the most extreme examples of transferred racism was when I was officially accused of assault by healthy, athletic white male college students. They had refused to speak to me directly about a disagreement and instead aired their unsubstantiated complaints on the student radio station. I confronted their passive-aggressive lies and unwillingness to have integrity (and I maybe even got a little loud). However, I never touched or threatened these tender children. As a result, I was given a leave of absence while their claims that they felt "threatened by my presence on campus" were investigated. Their lies about the assault were uncovered, yet I was mandated to apologize for "confronting them in a manner not consistent with the ethos…" of that particular college.

During my leave of absence from the college, my wife got a phone call reminiscent of what occurred in the movie 'Glory Road.' She answered the phone to hear '…n***er lovers – gonna f*** every one of you!' I wasn't even home at the time to comfort her. The next morning I contacted my supervisor, an African American man, to tell him. I said, "I don't want to make this public. But I want someone to know, just in case something happens." This was while I worked at a "Christian" college.

At another small college, I lost my position when I disclosed a primary source of institutional racism. As I stood accused, the one person who could have defended my assertions physically turned his head and looked away. He later apologized stating that he was afraid for his job as well, yet he realized all he needed to do was take the risk of acting as an advocate.

Often, brothers of color have jokingly warned me that even white folks, if they begin to speak out about prickly racial issues, can have their "white card" revoked. This has been my experience more than once. Solidarity with persons of color may lead to a diluting, and perhaps even the silencing of your voice in some circles.

My wife and I both found our faith severely tested after these experiences of racism and intolerance at Christian colleges. Our experiences were not unlike those of others who found hate and judgment in places where they were anticipating love and acceptance. At one time I felt that if the arrogant anger I was experiencing was the result of all the spiritual discipline being espoused; I wanted no part of it! However, the power of solidarity and community proved itself again as we both found healing through friends, multi-cultural bible study groups, and mentors. We have been encouraged and supported by people of color whose faith in Jesus is their "strength in the time of trouble" and not their ticket to cultural superiority and political position.

And so hope for a more just and loving community is the fuel that consumes silence and inspires action. Today, this same solidarity with Latinos gives me conviction and courage to advocate for fair and just immigration reform even though we have friends and family who are opposed to any reform that would give dignity and status to undocumented workers. But I cannot turn my back on a friend, just because he or she lacks the "documentation" that is arbitrarily given by a broken system.

Solidarity and credibility are sacred gifts and not ones I take lightly. Some say I'm an agitator. I hope I'm a reconciler, and would like to think I'm a peacemaker. I, too, wish we could all "... just get along" but there can be no real peace without justice. I love fellowship, I love a party, but don't invite me to eat at the table if all my friends can't come too!

Consider…

Have relationships across race or class ever caused existing relationships to suffer?

How have friendships across cultural barriers caused you to shift your social/political views?

How do you define "solidarity"?

Is it possible to be in solidarity with people of a different race or class? How or/how not?

What things need to be surrendered and/or obtained to be in true solidarity?

What can you do to assure that all are welcome at the tables you are part of?

Destined to BE …

Sittin' in Lulu's Jazz Café

Listen to R & B

Reading Boyd's book "The new HNIC"

I began to realize a thought that had - for some time

Been percolating in my soul…

I was destined to be a (hands-out) –

From days of being teased cuz I had big ***er-lips

Being mis-called and mis-used cuz the "q" in my name

Havin hair that won't feather or part like the others

I liked music with soul – more than rock and roll

I danced unrestrained and had no shame –

I was destined to be a (fist to chest) –

Had to learn not to care if I wasn't like everyone else

Had to learn ghetto survival skills of makin' do

getting' along wit what was there –

I had a late introduction to African-americans

A wrestler - Jr. high – curiosity – caught my eye

A strange sense of camaraderie but why?

Movies – shows – music and more

A connection to an unknown

But a destiny that God understood

Was being arranged for His good

Is it a Hip-Hop connection?

An urban culturalization?

Is it a soulful realization,

That we share more than we know

Don't categorize or castorize me

with narrow racist thinking

I'm not a wigger – culturally confused

Loathing my identity

Stealing a style for a season of comfort

No!

The browning of my soul

has been a life long journey

my epidermis does not reflect

the bronze that's been burned

deep within my consciousness

Yes,

I have security –

in the calling of eternity

Jesus set me free

time again – I've been saluted

"What up- my (fist in air)"

not a title I wear lightly –

But with honor and pride

Unable to return this

Compliment in kind –

I repay - by being willing

To be down –

Associated

Relegated

Denigrated

Yet elevated – wit my brothers

Not to serve

Not to save

But to suffer - And laugh

Cry and rejoice

that I am

By the grace of God

Yours (hands out)

Raising Children beyond the Color Line

As the Alabama sun beat down relentlessly on our little crew, curious onlookers observed that we were not your typical tourists. As we unloaded from our van, it was clear that we were purposeful, we were not somber, but we were focused on our goal. Young and old together are a unique sight most anywhere, but we looked even more out of place here in the heart of old Dixie. We were also black and white, together by choice.

We stood together at the National Civil Rights Memorial, the cool water flowing across the smooth granite looked inviting, but we knew this was no opportunity to play. Phil, our resident tour guide (and play-uncle-to-all) had instructed the adults and children alike what we were to do before approaching the slab of marble: "Choose a person from the memorial guide, read about their life and death, and then walk up and find their name chiseled into the stone."

We gathered around the granite table, our fingers tracing the names as water rippled over our hands and onto the ground. Behind us water also flowed over a wall with the inscription "… Until justice rolls down like waters and righteousness like a mighty stream" (Amos 5:24)

One by one, we shared. I chose, James Reeb, a white pastor who came to Selma from the north to help push for voting rights and was killed by an angry mob. My youngest son Tyler was about 10 years old. He carefully spoke the names he had chosen to share: Addie Mae Collins, Denise McNair, Carole Robertson, and Cynthia Wesley. All four were killed September 15, 1963 in the Birmingham church bombing. All were between 11 and 14 years of age. We each, it seemed, had chosen a person, or group, with whom we could identify.

On that trip my sons were confronted with the ugly power hate has to kill and destroy. But through our group experiences, we also saw the enduring power of love. Our strange little crew walked side-by-side, black and white, across the Edmund Pettis Bridge where 30 years earlier peaceful civil rights marchers had been beaten and tear-gassed by hateful and angry Alabama officers. We later had communion at a church in Selma and heard stories, from some who were there in 1965, of how God was beginning to heal the deep racial divides in that town.

We stood together at the site of the Montgomery slave auction block and considered the very different American history experiences behind the members of our group. Yet through it all, we saw how black, white, and brown could stand in love and begin to implode the power of hate that had been fed for years on a diet of stereotypes, prejudice, and disproportionate privilege.

This physical journey was a pivotal part of the spiritual and social journey my children and our family have made over the past 20 plus years. It was during this time I began to realize that some of the greatest benefits of raising our children in a multi-racial, urban setting might not occur in my life, but in the lives of my children and the generation we were helping to rear.

Live in fear, or live in engagement?

Over the past two decades, there have been times my wife and I have worried that maybe we were causing our children more harm than good by raising them in an urban/multi-cultural setting. We both come from a Midwest rural homogeneous environment. Our journey to the inner city was both by a sense of call and the privilege of choice. Yet, we never could have made it without the diverse community we were grafted into. This community was our source of wisdom and support.

For example, both our boys (in separate incidents) were singled out and robbed for their bikes. The most vivid and difficult for me was definitely the first time. It made me realize that if we were to live in the 'hood, it would be impossible to completely protect my children from their world. It would require me to guard my heart, trust God, and prepare them to be members of the society in which we were located. If we were to live here, we could not live in fear, but in engagement and solidarity with our community.

Jared, our oldest son, was about six or seven at the time. We didn't have a lot of money so we were thrilled to have been able to buy a sweet five-speed at a garage sale. He was so excited, not only did he have a new bike, but his grandpa and grandma from Iowa were visiting that day. He couldn't wait, so he rode up and down the sidewalk on our block.

Now, Grandpa and Grandma loved to have us visit them on the farm, and often subsidized our visits with free gas, beef and other rewards. We loved visiting them as well, and relished the chance to relax and enjoy county life. But for them to visit us in the city was a much greater "sacrifice." Not that they didn't visit, but they found themselves in a real conundrum; they hated everything about city life, yet loved us, and our urban friends.

Jared was a very trusting kid at that time; he hadn't yet developed "street sense," and I hadn't the sense to teach it to him. So when three older boys (10-12) asked him to show them where the park was at, he never suspected it was trap to get him away from the front of the house. Once they lured him to the corner, they knocked him over and made off with the shiny five-speed garage sale prize.

I was at the church office at that time, about 4 blocks away, so I don't know how he came back into the house; yelling, crying, or just mad. I just know I got a frantic call from Janeen. "Marque, some kids just stole Jared's bike. He's ok, but shook-up and mad." I hung up and ran out the back of the church. The fastest way home was in our 25 passenger church bus. On the way home, my anger grew into hatred for the unknown perpetrators. I "knew" they had picked on him because he was white, I "knew" they were black, and I KNEW racist feelings I thought had been crucified were being resurrected.

When I came up to the corner of our block, Jared was waiting for me. But he was not alone; Ralphe, Robert, and Lloyd were there too. They jumped into the bus and we cruised the neighborhood for almost 30 minutes. We were a posse looking to rain down justice on the evil bike thieves. We never did find them, probably by God's grace.

As I drove around with these neighborhood friends, who happened to be black and brown, and had willingly joined in to help their little "homie" get his bike back, my mind was forced to reconsider our place in this neighborhood, and my anger and my assumptions. Yes, this was a place that required special wisdom and skill to function and thrive. However, the rainbow of friends that surrounded us assured my son and me that race was not the sole defining factor of our role in the community; we were not the "white folks," we were friends and neighbors.

I later asked Jared what the kids who stole his bike looked like. He described height, clothes and approximate age. He only told me the "race" after I asked specifically, "…what color of skin did they have?"

"They had dark skin" he casually remarked. I asked Jared if that affected how he thought about other people with "brown-skin" – he just looked at me like I was crazy.

"Why…?" he asked, "It was just some stupid kids who take other people's stuff."

As I processed this with our church community, most all told stories of robbery, assault, and burglary. They also shared tips for safety, and keys for engaging the neighborhood in proactive ways. Our children were encouraged, comforted and challenged. We grew in struggle. Not by avoidance, but in a community of wisdom and support.

When my sons were in middle school another event shook their world. It was a neighborhood snowball fight that turned into a physical assault. An older black youth came out of the park gymnasium and saw the action. Through his own racial filters, he only saw an older white boy pelting smaller black boys with snowballs. Believing it was a racial attack he intervened with force. He grabbed my oldest son, picked him up, and threw him down on the ice-covered walkway. Calling him a racial slur, he threatened both my sons if they didn't "stop picking on black kids."

What he didn't expect was that all the kids (black, brown and white) would turn on *him* for attacking their friend. In spite of the physical pain, this experience gave my sons, and our community, an opportunity to see how the power of real relationships, forged in real-life struggles, supersedes the social barriers of race.

Through such experiences, friends and mentors of many races helped my children, and us, to guard hearts and minds from the poison of prejudice. This immunization process was not accidental. It goes back to intentional choices we made: Where we would live, what church we would attend and who the "extended family" that we invited into our lives would be.

Developing Racial Identity

All three of our children have a unique "initial awareness story" when it comes to race. As an educator, with some background in sociology, I had wondered about the development of racial awareness. I thought it would be a safe and interesting experiment to just let them live in a very diverse world and wait to see when, and how, they would discover the racial distinctions of this world.

I remember talking to my co-pastor, Nathaniel, about this. As a African-American parent, he informed me that my experiment itself was a privilege I had as a white man. He and his wife knew it would not be wise to let their children's racial awareness happen accidentally. They knew if they did not take preemptive action to teach their child about their racial and cultural identity, someone else (usually a white person) would take it upon himself or herself to inform them, and possibly degrade them in the process.

Our children grew up in three communities. First, there was the neighborhood they lived in. This was the almost all black/brown world. When they were in the backyard, out front riding bikes, or at the park, my kids were the splash of cream in the coffee. This was not just where they played but where most of my work was focused for the first 12 years in Minneapolis.

The second community was our church; we were an intentionally multi-racial community. While most of the youth were black and brown, there were more white young adults and families. Our leadership was pretty evenly mixed; it was a place where they saw racial issues addressed and dealt with in a healthy, not divisive, manner.

The third community was the world they would enter into when we would venture back to visit our families in the rural Midwest. This was a world that was almost all white. This was a place my children loved to visit, filled with the love and fun of grandparents and cousins, and yet it was a very strange place where "some people," for "some odd reason," just did not exist.

Because of these factors, each of our children had a unique journey toward racial awareness. For Jared, our oldest, there was that day when we returned with a van load of neighborhood kids from a trip to the zoo during spring break. When I got out of the van, I noticed him gazing deeply at his hands, front and back, front and back. "What's wrong?" I asked him. He looked at me like only an innocent kid can, and asked, "Why ain't my skin brown?"

Here was a white kid, not having the typical first awareness of race (that others are *not* white). He noticed that *he* was the different one. That spring trip, lead to a yearlong struggle of racial awareness for my five-year-old son. He spent from then until December asking Jesus if he could have brown skin for Christmas. We finally convinced him, by showing him photos of cousins and by visiting family, that he really was "ok." God had made him and there was nothing wrong with having "peachy" colored skin.

My next son, Tyler, vocalized his awareness of race about three years later. He was six years old at the time. We were walking through the neighborhood with his cousin from Iowa, on the way to our neighborhood park. Suddenly, without warning, he blurted out to me, "Why do only black people smoke?" His abrupt declaration reminded me that we lived in a predominately black community. I quickly looked to see who might have heard this junior bigot make such an inflammatory remark.

I tried to remain calm and un-judgmental as I answered him. "Why do you say that?" He looked at me, "I never see white people smoke." His Iowa cousin calmly said, "You should just spend more time in Clarksville, there are lots of people that smoke there."

The only "white people" he knew were family and church members, none of whom smoked. Yet he saw around him many people in the community (mostly black) who smoked regularly. His comments made me consider how natural it is for people to observe our racially segregated communities and quickly make pseudo–scientific evaluations that rationalize the differences and inequalities. My son's comments were not based on a bias against blacks, but came from a limited exposure to whites, resulting in unfair comparisons. This illustrates how deeply this "race illusion" impacts all levels of society. Why after six years of age is a child aware of race's power in social distinctions?

Our daughter Morgan is five years younger than her brother. Like the boys, she had a very diverse experience in her church and neighborhood. She went to head start where she was one of a few white kids in the entire school. One night after praying and tucking her in, she called me back into her room, and in her own innocent way asked, "Daddy, Dano has brown skin, and her momma an daddy got brown skin, but what color am me?"

Her reference to "brown" skin was not based on a "racial" distinction, but just an observation of human differences with no social stigma or power connected to those traits. She placed no value on certain colors of skin; at her age she had seen no relative advantages or disadvantages because of the color. She only wanted to understand.

I didn't want to immerse her into the world of the fake – but powerful - categories of black and white. So I just said, "Oh you're just kind of a peach–pink color – like your momma and me, and real cute too! Now just get to sleep, ok?"

Morgan continued to use the "brown" and "peach" categories well into her elementary years, and then someone had to tell her, "...no, its really black and white!"

For my children, the shadow of uncertainty that they felt in their small world vanished quickly as they became more aware of the wider (and whiter) world beyond North Minneapolis. For children of color, that shadow often grows and becomes more intimidating as they see the world beyond home is usually vastly different, and often outright hostile.

Lasting Impact

At the time of writing this, my sons are in college and in the workforce. They have never expressed regret for the experiences and exposure they had behind the color line as children. I am encouraged and occasionally surprised to see them as advocates and ambassadors for social and racial justice. They are more confident of who they are and what they want to be than I ever was at their age and are respected by both peers and adults of many races and classes. All our children are proud of their urban roots.

My daughter is in high school with a unique perspective on race, justice and God. At thirteen she played on a park league football team as a dual minority; the only girl and the only white kid. She has been part of a neighborhood track team with primarily African-American coaches and participants. She is well known and respected in our neighborhood and frequently takes the city bus. Morgan is respected in her public city high school as a leader and a uniter.

When people ask us about raising kids in the city, in a racially and socially diverse place, we have no easy answers or simple steps.

For our children diversity is not something they just see in movies. They have lived out the real struggles and seen the rich benefits of friendships in a community that crosses the social barriers most people seldom escape. Our children have had mentors and friends of many races and classes.

They know *people*: people of various races who defy the stereotypes often plastered on their communities. They know *people*; who may be the marginalized, the homeless, undocumented immigrants, drug addicts, and gang members. They are not social statistics but real people, and frequently family friends. They understand the destruction caused by drugs and gangs, as well as the social injustices that allow them to flourish. They have seen firsthand how the power of love - from a God of grace through people of purpose - can bring transformation to broken individuals and communities.

Some believe it is wise, in the name of "protecting their children" to keep them from the world of struggle and violence. Hence they seek to live far from others in social and cultural isolation. However, struggle and violence are usually symptoms of broken relationships and cannot be escaped through geography. Real safety then is found through building intentional communities, in which we live and grow, together by choice. Here the wisdom of diverse experiences enhances all. In this environment, the world with all its complexities, diversities, and ironies can be engaged. Cultural isolation will lead to fear and division. Multi-cultural engagement opens the door to Beloved Community.

Consider...

What do you think about the parenting decisions the Jensen's made?

Have you ever had an experience in which ugly racial attitudes, that you had thought were gone, came back to influence your thinking?

What to you is the balance between parenting that "protects our children FROM the world" and parenting that "prepares our children FOR the world?"

Are there risks involved in choosing to raise your family in a "safe" area? If so, what would those be?

How did your racial awareness develop?

What significant experiences helped shape that awareness?

The Least of These…?

Listen – Listen … Learn!

In love – together – we can discern,

How to Act to advance the Kingdom of God

Not deploy your personal escape POD

Escucha - Escucha … Aprende!

Listen – Listen … Learn!

In love – together – we can discern,

To Advocate in Solidarity

And live as his Beloved Community

YEA, I'm a cauk-asian – but my soul is brown

Don't wear this epidermis like a freakin' crown

I can comprehend Ebonics – flow in español

Si quieres ser loco – I'm ready to roll

Por mi gente – la raza – mi barrio o hood

Forget all them hatas say'n we up to no good

It's time to pull off the hood – do what we should.

500 years – white lies – we 'bout out of tries

The obsessions–the oppressions -

the lack of confessions,

Will we neva learn from our painful lessons?

The grace of god abounds – but we treat it like dirt

using wack-theology to band-aid the hurt

It's a damn shame people think Church is fake,

Neva would of happen if we lived 4 Jesus' sake!

Jesus' love compels – go and show

Not just front and floss 'bout what you know.

Listen – Listen … Learn!

To the least of these – Who's the least of these? We!

Not - What 'bout my stacks,

To do as I please.

What about the least of these?

———

Listen – Listen … Learn!

To The gang-banger, the kid who can't read

To the homeless mom with extra mouths to feed

To the working family with no health care

Or that "illegal alien" who snuck in over there

From the voices of those pushed to the side

Let the word of God be your guide

YEA, I'm a cauk-asian – but like John Brown

My souls been pierced by the colonized sound

20 plus years - earned a rep' – norf'side

For the 612 - I got real pride

From the church – to the streets –

and the schools wit no books

Survived the dealers- n – hookers – n – the cops dirty looks Yet "mookie –n da boys" know the meaning of respect

Most my beef - with 4-0 and the way he reflects

The attitude of hate – we learn and imitate –

Pride demonstrates and we fail to relate

So the rich get richer – the poor jus die –

Mine-apple – Calcutta? Who hears the cry?

Jesus' Love compels us to go and sho -

Not front and floss 'bout what you know

in a "Christian nation" - why can't kids read

Neva would of happen if we lived a kingdom creed

Listen – Listen … Learn!

To the least of these – The least of these?

We the least of these!

Not - What 'bout my stacks

To do as I please..

What about the least of these?

Listen - Listen – learn

From the voices of those pushed to the side

Let the word of God be your guide

Escucha – Escucha … Aprende!

Podemos avancar el reino de Dios

Si Escuchamos a los que no tienen una voz!

Listen – Listen … Learn!

In love – together – we can discern

To Advocate in Solidarity

And live as his Beloved Community

White Privilege:
A Journey of Initiation and Awareness

Not that many years back, I was appalled at the idea of white privilege. I knew how hard my dad had worked to turn a run-down farm into a place of beauty. I knew how his family had been dust-bowled off of the Nebraska plains and how both his parents died when he was only 16 years old. White privilege? No way! He worked hard for everything he got. To me, "white privilege" seemed like a way to blame white folks for what they had achieved; make us feel guilty and let minorities play the victim and blame others for their own failures.

Then my world turned upside down. Moving from the farm into the city and from a mono-cultural to a multi-cultural society, opened my eyes to many realities. I began to see and feel how real racism, prejudice and discrimination are, even in this modern, Obama era.

Let me give you a small example; I could drive with a cracked windshield and not worry about getting stopped; while my black brothers would not take a similar chance. They had learned that plenty of prejudiced police are looking for *any* reason to stop and question them.

I know some reading this will dismiss this example and say, "I'm sure they did something wrong to get stopped." For years, I tried to say that, too. But after enough experience with my urban friends, I could not continue to believe that racial profiling and unequal treatment were simply a matter of an overly sensitive imagination or victim mentality.

A significant part of my journey to understanding began with the awareness that white privilege is *NOT* about me getting something I didn't deserve – but about some people (because of their race and culture) *NOT* getting the same opportunities.

First hand experiences have shown me that White Privilege is not a ridiculous tool used to blame whites and excuse minority failure, nor is White Privilege just about a few isolated individual experiences.

White Privilege is a social reality that is the cumulative result of the consistent institutional and social rewards that whites give and receive, usually without awareness or intentionality. Simultaneously, these "rewards" are frequently, passively or actively, NOT afforded to blacks and other minorities. In short, not everyone gets the same opportunities or respect in day-to-day life. We all can cite a time we got unfair treatment, but for non-whites, across the social spectrum, this in-equality is something consistently experienced, resulting in fewer opportunities and more disrespect.

Imagine that we all are going on a hiking trip with packs, tents and supplies. I go to the outfitters and the workers help me get my gear together. They show me how to pack and what to bring. They supply me with quality, or at least satisfactory, equipment.

I head out and notice I am passing up people who are trying to carry their gear in paper sacks and some in worn out, sub-standard, backpacks. I notice some of the people I pass have even brought some gear that is unnecessary and slows their progress. They are getting frustrated and start complaining, their presence makes the trip less and less enjoyable. In my frustration I begin to blame "those people" for slowing *my* hike. I'm trying to make my way down the road. I begin to mumble to myself, "I carry my own gear, take care of my own stuff; why can't they do the same?" And, "why did *you* bring that ugly quilt and that salty attitude?"

Then I see the problem: the people struggling with oversized blankets, bulky tents and paper sacks never made it to an outfitter. I begin to ask why, and I learn that some didn't know the outfitter was there, some couldn't afford the service, and some tried, but were not even allowed to go into the outfitter's shop.

The unfairness of the whole situation is clear. It is unfair *not* because I went to an outfitter and found the support I received.

The injustice is that other people were arbitrarily denied access; either through lack of information, experience, or outright prejudice – to the resources I took for granted and assumed all would be able to obtain.

In preparation for the journey, I was privileged. It was not my fault, no one gave me something "special." It was the fact that what I took for granted was systematically denied to others based on criteria they could never meet.

White Privilege took on new meaning when I met Les. Les is a "First Nation," Native American man, or as he calls himself, an American Indian. When I first met him in the back alley of our church, he was pushing a grocery cart full of crushed cans. Les never saw himself as unemployed, he had a job, "canning." Now if you grew up gardening, you might think you know what canning is; this is not what I'm talking about. Les's job was picking up and recycling cans from off the streets.

In addition, Les never saw himself as homeless; he bragged that he had a "great camp site" where he stayed with a group of friends under the raised part of interstate 394 near Dunwoody Institute.

Les had a passion to follow Jesus. He had faith and love for God and others, a profound knowledge of scripture, and he was a chronic alcoholic. For over a year he seldom missed church on Sunday, and usually came by a few times during the week to talk over a cup of coffee and conversation, to pray, read, and maybe take a shower.

During these times Les and I often shared stories of our life. Les was an amazing storyteller. I began to realize that as different as our lives are today – there was a time when our ancestor's histories overlapped briefly, and then began to move in opposite directions.

In the 1870 – 1880's, a young man named Jorgen Jensen was looking for new opportunities in life. Life as a farmhand on his small Danish Island did not appeal to him. The German chancellor, Otto Von

Bismarck, had conquered that part of Denmark, and Jorgen, a proud Dane, did not want to serve in the army of the Iron Chancellor of Germany.

Jorgen had heard about the promises of America, and even though he had never heard of Nebraska, he decided to risk all and go. Perhaps he saw a poster at the church, town hall, or maybe a notice in a local paper, promising cheap, yet fertile land in America. Leaving his fiancé behind, he made the journey and began farming in Nebraska. After a few years, his wife-to-be joined him in establishing their home. They were the grandparents of my father.

Jorgen worked hard and nothing was given to him. He could have died in the harsh conditions. His first winter in Nebraska was the same harsh winter Laura Ingalls Wilder wrote of in *"The Long Winter."* The snows that year came early, blizzards were frequent, the cold was extreme and many prairie settlers perished. Jorgen had to bring his horse into his home which was dug-out into the hillside to keep them both from freezing to death.

In later years, Jorgen's son took over the farm. During the dustbowl/depression years he and his family struggled to survive. Drought conditions left them with no crops year after year. During WW2, many family members left for military jobs in Seattle. My dad's family eventually left the farm in Nebraska to move to Iowa.

The pioneer spirit, which was born from opportunities and challenges, persevered and was passed on generation to generation. The family learned how to succeed, even in the midst of hardships. Jorgen's grandson also knew that same optimism and drive. It was that faith in hard work and fairness that my dad passed on to me.

In the 1870's war and political ambitions were being waged in the USA which also transformed Nebraska. All states west of the Mississippi River were being cleared of the native "Indian" population. This was done by treaty and by war; and the United States Government always got its way.

During this time, Les's great-grandparents, like mine, were going through experiences that would change their lives and the lives of their offspring forever. To make room for new settlers from Europe, they were forced off their land. A way of life they had known for generations was destroyed as they were forced to live on reservations where their life and culture were stripped away. These families, unlike my grandparents, had no opportunity for risk, reward and adventure; they were forced into the conditions of a conquered people.

Christian missionaries were sent as agents of the state to "domesticate the savages." To accomplish this, children were forcibly removed from their parents and sent to boarding schools. Here they were punished for speaking their native language and the European-American lifestyle was imposed them. The stated mission of the boarding schools was to, "kill the Indian and save the child." Native children were not allowed to feel pride about their ancestry, yet were denied citizenship in the new country to which they were expected to assimilate.

Neither equal protection under the law, nor love as fellow humans was extended to Les's family and the millions of others from the First Nations of this land. This was not a mission of Jesus' love and grace, but of enforcing a national goal of manifest destiny via conquest and removal.

The result was anger, shame and frustration. To this day the feelings of inferiority and resentment continue to besiege life on the reservation and are at the heart of the high levels of depression, poverty, chemical abuse, and suicide.

Les's grandparents loved and cared for him, yet were unable to give him the optimism and faith my grandparents passed to me. This is the legacy of a nation structured around the principles of racial myth and the resulting privilege that is bestowed on those of the dominant group. On the plains of Nebraska, this drama unfolded as it did over and over across the nation. The opportunities, challenges, and sense of worth that my great-grandfather gained from cheap land and a welcoming community came at direct cost to Les's family. They paid through pain, loss of pride and identity. Optimism and faith shrivel and wilt where depression and despair take root.

White privilege cannot be dismissed as just a term used by the liberal elite. It is a reality and a key concept to understand the racial and class dynamics we see around us today.

In the public television series "Race the Power of an Illusion", Dr. Beverly Tatum concludes with a discussion on how we are all born into a system that we did not create, nor ask to be part of. She emphasizes that shame and blame, will not change the realities and disparities around us.

Instead she points out that we need to ask the following questions:

- *What can I influence?*
- *How am I making this a more equitable environment?*
- *Who is included in this picture and who isn't?*
- *Who has had opportunities in my environment and who hasn't?*
- *What can I do about that?*

If you are a white person reading this, please wrestle with these questions. There are two extremes one can go to in considering white privilege. The one is denial. The other is self-hatred. Neither will help address the issues of privilege and the resulting inequalities. In my community, and in myself, I have recognized that few things can harm a diverse community more than white folks who hate themselves. Sure, one must seriously grieve the injustice of privileges given based on race. However, to take this to a point of self-loathing, leaves one impotent as an agent for change. To summarize Dr. Tatum, "you didn't ask for this position, but how can you leverage it to help level the playing field?"

At the same time, do not forget that "racially enlightened" white people are *not* the saviors of people of color. In fact, the *savior* attitude is possibly more damaging than a denial of privilege. Awareness of privilege (and the refusal to blindly participate in the system it creates) opens the door in this Hip-Hop, post-civil rights era to be a partner in the quest for Beloved Community

The ability, even the importance, of an honest critic of culture by whites as they enter into dialogue and community with persons of color is echoed by Michael Eric Dyson, Professor at Georgetown University, in an insightful book on Hip-Hop culture, "Know What I Mean?"

Dyson writes:

> "Color can't be the basis for analyzing culture because some of the best insight on black folk has come from white brothers and sisters. ... But there is something to be said about the dynamics of power, where nonblacks have been afforded the privilege to interpret and – given the racial politics of the nation - legitimate and decertify ... in ways that have been denied to black folk. ... So it's not simply a question of the mastery of a set of ideas... it's also about the power to shape a lens through which this culture is interpreted..." (p. 4)

This underscores the reason that whites must first acknowledge the history and presence of power if we hope to help shape a new racial/political conversation. We must forge this conversation together being aware of our own baggage that needs to be left behind, and yet willing to help carry the baggage of another, if need be.

To persons of color reading this, may I humbly offer my opinion? I believe we all must ask the same questions Ms. Tatum articulates above. My friends of color in this journey have consistently demonstrated to me how one can move beyond blame and become part of the solution. These leaders seek to engage all, regardless of race, for the building of communities that overcome our racist legacy.

Most persons of color I've known are open and gifted in building and working across race. However at times I have observed two unproductive extremes that can hinder the destruction of racism and white privilege. The one is blind blame and anger at the racist inequality many struggle with daily. The other is blind participation in this individualistic, and systemically racist system to "*get mine*" and "*get out.*" Sure I understand the rationale for these extremes, but they both end in isolation and do nothing to help facilitate the building of Beloved Community.

Most importantly, it is rarely *my job* to tell another what they should do to "fix" the problem. However, it is always my job to make sure I am doing *my part*. If I do that with an intentional consistency, trust will develop, which in turn may allow others to enter into a relationship where they can begin to see how they can contribute to the solution.

To learn to own, or confront, privilege in our world we must come to terms with the Apostle Paul's words.

> "…there should be no division in the body, but … its parts should have equal concern for each other. If one part suffers, every part suffers with it; if one part is honored, every part rejoices with it." (1 Corinthians 12: 25b – 26)

One defining quality of a Beloved Community is that it naturally mourns and celebrates as one; A place where no one can enjoy privilege alone while another grieves alone. White privilege cannot be ignored, nor can it be embraced. It must be engaged in a way that begins to dismantle it, while at the same time channeling its inertia to help empower the very ones it was designed to leave behind.

Consider...

How do you define white privilege?

Have you seen or experienced the direct impact of racial privilege? How? Where?

Do you think it is fair for Marque to link his and Les' great-grandfather's experiences with their present conditions?

How did racial policies of the past impact your family?

What do you think about Ms Tatum's comments?

What part can/do people of color play in dismantling the systems of white privilege?

What can white people do about privilege as they seek a more just world?

What is the role of persons of color in helping to dismantle the power of white privilege and insure equal opportunity and access for all?

I know IT is there..

I do not know how to explain it

But I know I am a fool not to NAME it

Like the air we breathe

It permeates, penetrates,

The interactions – demonstrations

Of who we are and how we rate

Invisible fences - unwritten rules -

White privilege

defines the victors – predestines the fools

I know there are exceptions - but they are "excepts" –

That confound the typical – break the statistical

But the system is programmed to self- correct

White is not a color of skin –

even the un-tanned booty of your caucasian cousin ain't white

YET- Even the darkest brown brother

from the mother land ain't true black

White and black with hues of brown in between

were never simple descriptors

But power broker labels –

status bestowing - bastardizing constructs

For colonizing , patronizing,

Dehumanizing power to destruct

Divide and conquer – Greed based theology –

Creating God in MY image – ethnocentric Christology

To keep my Tower of Babel secure and un-scattered

I build monuments to MY kind

and MY image un-tattered

No place for Divine revelation, or YOUR kind's contamination.

White Privilege…

is the atmosphere our culture has created

In this- we live and move and find our being

We inhale it's blessings, curses …

Allergens – and rote verses

To some it is fresh air

Empowering and assuring

It is invisible - rarely noticed, but always enduring

But if suddenly –

Stripped away, altered, or exposed

Those dependent on it's presence gasp and groan,

Threats - guilt

They blame their discomfort on those who

Lowered the pressure

Changed the components

Of the atmosphere on which their life is built.

Can we consider life without the reassuring winds?

That the world of western imperialism

was not God's design but man's whims?

For countless others

this atmosphere daily is filled with the allergens

that lead to doubt – identity confusion

Marginalization – prejudging whole nations

Based not on reality – but the race illusion

Consistent discomfort - a chronic condition

Blame self for the reactions that lead to shortness of breath–

But could it be in response to the air you breathe,

Or are others really more and you are just less?

You need filters just to survive –

Many light skinned brothers think

It is just something you contrive

When they see you in gas mask on *their* sunny day

And you get blamed for causing the drama –

when you jus tryin to live when each breath brings trauma

A mirror image of white privilege is apt to appear

Born out of anger – born out of fear

Brown bitterness

Reflects the deficits

Of justice and peace

A cycle as losses and injury increase

But Brown Bitterness, the image in the mirror

Is it only as large as the object of terror?

Are we helpless victims?

or passive participants?

Can we color the climate – to help others visualize

White privilege – can I fight U?

Can I renounce U – can I use U?

Can we drain the bubble?

Live in a place where the impacts bring less trouble-

When White privilege loses power and control

Will Brown Bitterness lose it's grip on the soul?

White Privilege

I know U are there

I do not know How to explain it

But I know I am a fool not to NAME it

I can BE – undefined by U

I can BE ME - free of your power

I can resist – insist we include the missed

I can BE grace and truth without MY tower

How ???

No easy 3-step process exists

No short-cut to bliss

But the path we are on

Is bound to miss

Without risk and sacrifice.

Obedience and love

Relationships and faith can make:

Theory become family

Abstractions become connections

Religion becomes real

And privilege,

Becomes something

I can never enjoy alone

If my siblings are left out –

and I claim Christ is on the Throne.

Siento Enojado (I Feel Angry)

Siento enojado – cuando pienso de los malvados

Los sin corazones, con caras falsas

que sienten nada buena por mi gente de la raza.

Ellos hablan mucho de los cosas no entienden

y no quieren por las familias ellos están ofenden

ANGER, I feel @ hard hearted folks – talking smack about what they don't know – offending families as they babble like these broke laws come direct from GOD

Sin amor y compasión ellos hablan de "ilegales"

ellos creen el ley del mundo es el final de los reglas.

Hay un ley y un Señor – mas allá de un país

de familia, amor, paz. Agua y maíz.

Porquel mundo es de el Señor

– no hay gente ilegales.

Yo dijo, las fronteras existen

solo para defender sus ganas.

Si, yo entiendo, soy un hijo del poderoso padre,

también, entiendo ellos son de mi sangre, solo de una otra madre!

Oh yea, God did NOT make boarders –

greedy people did,

We are all children of a Father almighty

of the same blood

brothers and sisters –

seeking a way in a messed-up world

If people are criminals, arrest them –

But trying to care for your family,

survival isn't a crime – it is heroric -

Claro que si, algunos gente hacen hechos mal

Y por eso necesitamos la policía – como luz y sal

Pero el demasiado de la gente sin papeles,

No están criminales -

¡No son héroes!

Trabajando por sus familias ,

en reverencia y humildad.

Buscando por la voluntad de Dios,

cuando los duros viven en oscuridad

I will cry out with the voice of old and the revolution!

For the people, justice, love and liberty!

¡Voy gritar!

Como la voz de antiquidad

¡Por la gente!

¡Justicia!

¡Amor y libertad!

Making Peace with Mestizo

On this past Cinco De Mayo we went to a local club to hear several Minnesotan-Mexican Hip-Hop groups. It was, as the saying goes, da-bomb! We helped start a dance-cipher with the lead MC of one group, we had banners and flags to wave that had been tossed from the stage. I even was handed the mic to help rap the hook, "*a la raza en la casa...*" during the final free-style-everybody-on-the-stage-cut. Several times during the night I was asked a question a frequently hear, "...de donde eres, Puerto Rico? Argentina? Mexico? Cuba?" and if I don't say it first one of my friends will say "Heck no, el es puro gringo!"

Friendships with Mexicans and other Latinos have altered the trajectory of my life and mission. Trust and earned credibility, again leave their mark. I never had a class in Spanish. I believe my ability to speak is a gift from God that mirrors the friendships I've been given. My experience also reflects the national and global trend of mestizaje, described by Father Virgilio Elizondo in "The Future is Mestizo."

Mestizo means "mixed" or literally "half-breed." Elizondo believes that the mixing of cultures that he has witnessed in his home of San Antonio is the hope for our future, God's desire for us. During colonization, this was not the case. Mestizo was the result of the oppression and violence brought with the conquistadores.

To be mestizo carried with it the weight of shame, a class that was constantly being reminded that they could not fully participate in either culture. However, over time, mestizo became normalized. The mix of Spaniard with the First Nations of Mesoamerica, created a new culture and people. Elizondo observed how this same process was at work in his home of south Texas. He concludes by stating that in a world of mestizaje, "Differences are not being destroyed, but they are being transcended and celebrated as together we usher in the beginning of the new race of humanity... a united family..." (p 111)

I've seen a taste of this reality from the streets of Minneapolis and other US cities to Warsaw and Berlin, and to the south in cities of Mexico, Guatemala and Honduras. At times I've seen it in the church. Yet, you are much more likely to experience this united family through street culture and Hip-Hop, which is much more inclusive and less judgmental than much of the logical, left brained, religious institutions that forgot to do the "right" thing.

I was reminded of this recently when I tuned my radio dial to a station I quit listening to years ago. They could have embraced the mestizo reality of the Christian community. They had started down that path, but they retreated into the world of stale white-bread with no peanut butter or jelly.

When they met resistance to a slightly mestizo-ized play list from their core audience (Jane the suburban white soccer-mom), they retreated into mono-culturalism by cutting all voices of color. Such real life experiences are normal. Dominant white culture trains us to reject whatever does not fit into the paradigms of prescribed sociology or theology. However I find God is not colorblind, the creator enjoys human diversity, is not bound to defend whiteness, nor is God limited by our cultural biases.

In 1984 I made my first trip to Mexico. It could have been anywhere in the world where poverty smacks you in the face and clobbers the conscience, but I went to Mexico. I was a newlywed and I drove a bus of donated clothes to a border mission in Laredo, TX. We went into Mexico only once on that trip and I was stunned at the extreme poverty just a stone's throw from the USA. I swore I would come back.

Three years later I was in a different border town, Piedras Negras, with a group of youth from South East Christian Church. We assisted a church with construction and outreach. It was a powerful experience and it was there I met a friend, Armando Contreras. He was the youth pastor of the church and would become a brother to me; eventually coming to college in Rochester, living with my family in Iowa, and bringing me to his home town of Monterrey, MX, countless times.

On our last night together, during that first visit to Piedras Negras, the church held a large youth rally. We played games, worshipped, ate and had some of the sweetest fellowship. Our multiracial youth from Minneapolis and the members of this community were together as brothers and sisters. As the night wore on we left the church building and gathered around a bonfire. There we talked and sang until dawn began to break across the North Mexican desert sky.

Off in the distance I saw the lights of McDonalds. We had extra money in our budget; I knew what we could do! Let's load everyone up in our van and a few other cars – we could all go get breakfast under the Golden Arches. We could buy for everyone as our farewell gift.

I proudly announced what WE could do. I began to waken those who had drifted off to sleep. I was excited for a Sausage McMuffin… but I noticed something strange: most of the Mexican youth suddenly had reasons they needed to go home. I asked my new friend Armando, "Why is everyone leaving?" He looked at me "Marcos, ellos no pueden venir; esta en el otro lado" "Marque, they can't come; it's on the other side"

I was heartbroken – why can't my friends eat McMuffins with me?

I was angry – what right does a river have to say who can cross and who can't?

I was embarrassed – why didn't I think before I talked?

My journey into Latino culture has constantly prodded my ignorance and dismantled my assumptions. This was just the beginning. A connection was being made, a web was being spun, that I could not easily escape. I wrestled with the stark disparities between the USA and Mexico. I was confronted with our obscene wealth vs. the obscenity of abject poverty. Yet while I was in Mexico I seldom felt pity *for* the people and I almost always felt welcome *from* the people. There, I was invited to partake in a refreshingly real community. Seemingly, away from the pressures of materialism that constrict us here in the USA. We were able to reflect on the basics and the essentials of life in the context of a community that modeled love and peace.

Soon we found ourselves preparing for a trip a little deeper into Mexico, to Monterrey, Armando's hometown. He was attending college in Minnesota, and knew of countless opportunities for us there, besides, he wanted us to meet his friends and family. That first trip opened up opportunities and experiences that have profoundly changed many lives.

After a fulfilling yet tiring week, we left Monterrey on a rainy night, most of the group quickly fell asleep. As we drove through the dimly lit streets, tears began to stream down my face. Mexican worship songs played on our tape-deck and I gazed at the people in the streets. I couldn't imagine life in the homes I was seeing, homes that provided less protection than barns in the USA. Yet I had made friends from such places. It was not the poverty that called us back, again and again to Mexico. It was the warmth and wealth of the friendships we had experienced. "I had to return, I could NOT forget."

I kept that vow for over 15 years. Almost every year, we would made a trip, some years even two. Occasionally I traveled there alone to prepare for our next group. Each time I learned more Spanish, and on each return I swore I'd keep studying. We formed deep relationships with Armando's family, the Contrerras'. Across Monterrey on the large hill of Topo Chico we forged lasting friendships with Pastor Nacho's (Ignacio) family, the Martinez-Leos'.

For a while I perused the idea of moving our whole family to Monterrey. I had a great idea; we would buy a house with a store on the first floor. Janeen and the kids would run the store. For income I would teach English to the wealthier residents who worked for the multi-national corporations. But our real purpose for living there would be to be involved in the church and community building. As much as I embraced that idea, Janeen dissuaded me; I now see that was a good thing.

As I look back on those years, I know God used that time for greater purposes. For one thing, the pastors and churches of Mexico taught me a great deal about holistic community building that I was able to bring back to Minneapolis. We also witnessed the transformative power of cross-cultural relationships as African-American youth from urban America connected with the urban Mexican youth and together they reveled in all they shared in common. The black students from the USA would often make comments of how freeing it was to be in Mexico, away from the "race-roles" they felt thrust upon them at home. I observed the benefits as my own children began to know peers, friends, who lived in poverty and forged relationships that shaped their understanding of their role in this world. It seemed as if God was preparing us for all the Mexicans and other Latinos that he would soon bring to Minneapolis.

During this time, my sons began attending a charter school, Cyber Village Academy. We were working with the school administrator to make the school more accessible to kids in our neighborhood. We had plans to provide bussing and allow students to use our church building as a site for a computer lab where kids could come to study. During one of my meetings with the administrator of the school, he noted that I spoke a fair amount of Spanish, he also knew I was a licensed schoolteacher. He made me an offer that, little did I know, would help me both with my Spanish and my computer skills. He asked if I would come teach Spanish to the 4 – 8th graders in the school.

About this same time, Armando pronounced me "fluent," however I knew I still had so much to learn. Teaching would be my greatest opportunity to learn. The first year was easy: games and songs, words and phrases. However all the students began asking for me to teach them the alphabet, and I didn't even know it. I had learned Spanish like kids learn any language; by sound and repetition. I knew the vowels and the sounds of the letters, but now I had to fill in the gaps and learn more systematically. I learned the ABC's; I learned more and more grammar, I worked on my spelling and reading – so I could teach the kids in my classes.

I had met some Mexican guys playing soccer in my neighborhood park. They invited me to play with them, which was putting them at risk of injury. My athletic training was primarily in wrestling and American-Football, so the finesse of soccer didn't come easy. I quickly learned what was "sucio" or dirty, and what was "limpio." I'm not the biggest guy, but with this group of Mexicans I was too big to be charging into "mis compañeros." But they were patient, and we had a blast. For this reason, if you play soccer with me, my first language on the field is Español… "buen tiro," is much more natural than "good shot". Needless to say, playing competitive sport my vocabulary grew in other ways as well. I won't repeat those words now but they have served their purpose well.

Several of the guys I played with began to ask if we knew of places they could learn English. At that time there were no classes being offered on the Northside. Soon our church was offering classes; volunteers from the church and local colleges came to assist. One problem we encountered was that most of the people in our class were struggling with a literacy-based approach to language learning. It was difficult for them to take notes, make flashcards or read the worksheets. We realized most of them were not fluent in reading Spanish, so how could they use written Spanish to learn English? The second issue is that most of the students were men while most of the tutors were women. Some didn't seem to mind the opportunity to talk with a nice gringa, but for others there was the issue of "machismo." There is the attitude with some that a real man shouldn't be taught by a woman.

At this time we landed on a model we used for over three years, and hope to do again soon. We called it Relational-Reciprocal; Language Learning. We would partner native English and Spanish speaking persons together, each wanting to learn the other language and each coming to teach their own language. The classes quickly grew and each week we would have large group sharing and listening and then each small group would pick-up on topics of interest.

An intern from Crown College, Chris Wood, and his wife Tatum, came to join us, he had been raised in Ecuador and she was a

Californian born Latina. Our next move was to offer bi-lingual worship services in which we mixed English and Spanish together in the worship, and then translated the sermon. It was a time of amazing growth and transformation for our small church and it pushed us to look at the paradigms of race, reconciliation, and unity from a much broader perspective; no longer were we a bi-racial church, but a multi-racial community.

Along the journey described in this chapter, something strange happened; people who I, at one time, considered much different from myself became true friends. John Perkins, founder of the Christian Community Development Association and a living legend of real reconciliation, says that friendship "has to do with seeing something of high value in someone, and must be based on true equality." As these Mexican and central-American men and women trusted me as a friend they began to share their fears, their stories, their hopes and their lives. We shared holidays in our homes. Their gift of friendship drew me to deeply consider what "equality," as Perkins spoke of it, would demand from me, and what it would give to me.

Over the last few years, I have felt both deep grief and fear watching the growing anti-Mexican and Latino movement in the USA. The most terrifying part of this is the level of anger coming from "Christians." Why conservative talk show hosts have more influence on the masses than the sacred scriptures is perplexing. Many evangelical Americans want nothing to do with mestizo. To them the conservative appeals to legalistic exclusion and isolation are comforting; the seeming brown and black invasion is disturbing. I was once one who was swayed by the fear talk. But I have tasted something more powerful, love and friendship, amor y amistad.

This is why I go to marches for immigration reform, blog and speak out about issues regarding the Latino community: my brothers and sisters. We share solidarity in humanity and in faith, so I will gladly join my voice with theirs to address injustice. Many of my "old friends" believe these changes, my peace with mestizo, are one more sign I've lost touch with my roots and betrayed my own. I see it as proof that God has taken hold of my heart and has allowed me the gift of new friendships.

I was recently at conference on reconciliation at Duke University. While there discussing immigrations issues, I met a young Latino man from New York City. A few days into the conference he came up to me and introduced himself, "Where you from, man?" "Minnesota," I replied.

He was unsatisfied, "But like, your parents; where they from?"

"Iowa, Nebraska, and before that Northern Europe," I stated.

He laughed, "Man, I would have sworn you were Latino or something. I got a friend who has one white and one Mexican parent, You look just like him, even sound a little like him too."

As Virgilio Elizario speaks of the hyphenated, mestizo people of today he reminds his readers that all great cultures, from the earliest civilizations of Africa, to the Aztecs and Spanish, the British, and most of the world, have grown and developed only as they made room for the best of others while clinging to the best of their own in order to become something even better. I have not become less because of my Mexican brothers; they have made me more, and I pray that in some small way I have returned the favor.

Consider ...

What experiences have you had that allow you to explore and learn other cultures?

Discuss the negative and positive side of "meztizo" both in the current and historical context.

How does friendship into a culture translate into solidarity with a culture?

What are human issues that you are concerned about today that you didn't care about in the past? What made the change?

BLACK ROBES and POMP ...
in a WORLD of DESPAIR

I was there to support students I had worked with as they were awarded their Bachelor Degrees. Many of them were first generation college graduates. I was excited for them, yet I was unable to focus. I was physically present, yet mentally I was across town. My mind was preoccupied; a young man who had been a student in my 10th grade World History class was dead, a victim of misdirected gang violence.

Sitting in the well-funded private college auditorium I couldn't help but be aware of a poignant juxtaposition. Here students lack nothing when it comes to the tools for their education, yet less than 10 miles away kids struggle in schools without adequate text books. I mused, "how can we have such abundance and such disparity within the same community? Or, are we NOT a comm*unity*?

Then I noticed the long lines of black robes with colored markings. They wound their way through the aisles and to the platform. At times I've been an active participant in this ritual, this time I was just an observer. But, for some reason I began to wonder what it had to do with anything remotely related to the kingdom of God.

My thoughts launched in a million directions. I've read that in the Kingdom the "last will be first" and that, "the greatest among you is the servant." This ritual seemed focused on what separates more than on what unites; there was the appearance that distinctions of education were the essence of status and value. Was there any reason to consider Jesus' warning of those who, "*make their phylacteries wide and the tassels on their garments long; they love the place of honor at banquets and the most important seats in the synagogues; they love to be greeted with respect in the marketplaces and to have people call them 'Rabbi."* (Matthew 23: 5-8) So... does that apply to wanting to be called "Doctor?"

Now, don't hear this as an attack or criticism; I'm not even sure what I think, I'm just sharing with you the thoughts that went through my mind. But to better help you understand what is going on IN my mind – let me begin by explaining what has gone INTO my mind.

I spent the first half of my life living on a farm; hard work and productivity were what mattered. Education was good, but it's "not worth a lick if you don't know how to work." The community that raised me had little regard for people who were smooth talkers or nice writers, if they were idiots when it came to being able to provide for themselves with an "honest day's work." Honest work meant you produced something of value. To most people that meant you could eat it, live in it, drive it or touch it. Along with productivity, the other enduring value in my prairie community was community connection and compassion. The only thing worse than being lazy and unproductive, was to be aloof; disconnected from the community, and unable to connect and care for those around you.

Academic parades and powerful degrees appear to be foolishness in this world where all that really matters is hard work and good, caring friends.

I've spent the last half of my life in another community where compassion and connectedness are also highly esteemed, the Northside of Minneapolis. Like the farm community in Iowa it really doesn't matter to folks what schools you've attended, articles you've written, or degrees completed. That all might be okay; but if you can't be trusted, if you're too busy trying to look good and forget to "do" good, if you are stuffy, fake or undependable - no one is impressed.

Urban communities also value productivity. But the struggles of life often prove to be a more powerful and destructive force than the desire to produce. There is really no more laziness in the city than in the country, there are just more good reasons for people to give up trying. It takes great strength to not give up fighting against what appear to be the impossible odds of class, race and educational disparities. Academic parades and powerful degrees can appear to be selfish vanity in this world where what matters most is survival and real friends that help you through.

I see these paradigms at work in both America and around the world. The truth is, most of the world does not have the luxury of caring what educational status one has. Parades in colorful robes seem foolish at best to the world's masses who are preoccupied with the "mundane" issues of daily survival. To these, such pomp is merely another example of the very waste and vanity that perpetuate the inequality and injustice that daily threaten their survival. My thoughts are not about a particular institution, but about the thousands that perpetuate these practices that seemingly value *vanity over substance.*

Parades of Black Robes with bright colors can demonstrate that one may be out of touch with humanity and yet create systems and rituals to validate their vanity and perpetuate petty piety. Are these not the people whose systems and theories maintain the status quo and promote capital growth at the expense of human development? Are they doing anything to make the world a better place to live?

While many of the robed ones seek profits over justice perhaps some can become prophets for justice. They can merely display their pomp and position, or they can use their power to "flip the script" and re-write the plot lines of the world.

The parades and black robes are foolish – unless they remember the people who most distrust them. If they remain connected to the masses of the world, they may be able to act on its behalf; if not, they will just look silly and vain to those who live in a reality of pain.

Those of us who have worn the black robes must not forget that we *will* lose touch if we ever cease to listen to the voices of those who already think that we have.

Consider...

What are the paradigms of values and desirable traits in your community?

What aspects of Marque's critique on academics do you agree?

What is the role of pomp and titles?

How can we bridge the disconnect between "real life and the academy?

Why is it that isolated academic activities become out of touch with the world?

Do you see people who have distrust or even disdain for academics?

What roles can academics play in a world of injustice? (Positive and negative)

How do your academic experiences influence your ability to connect with others? Does it make it easier or more difficult?

Sangre por Sangre

It wasn't the kind of place where good evangelical Christians were supposed to go. However, on this night, God *was* there, as the Prince of Peace to lead and protect. This is the Jesus who was more concerned about being present to the situation around him, than about protecting his reputation. To be a peacemaker, I learned is not a passive title, but to respond to an active call of duty.

Sure, it was a "church-sponsored" event, but since there was beer and dancing some would say it was a place to avoid, not a "Christian atmosphere" I was invited to this fundraiser for the immigrant community in a local small town. I was honored to be the guest of my friend, Andre, his 3 cousins, his great aunt and her boyfriend.

When first we arrived at Amvet Hall, the main room was filled with people of all ages. Men, women, and a few older children were all gathered together. Norteño, Duranguense, y Meringue music was pulsing, voices were loud and cheerful and the dance floor was filled to capacity. As we squeezed past the bar area, my friend ordered a round of Coronas and we slid into the annex. It was a small room off to the side, partially separate, but connected by a large door and an opening cut through the wall. From our vantage point, we could sit, talk and watch the crowd.

The DJ knew how to get and keep a party going; play good dance music, and don't talk too much. Talk enough to remind people why they were there, to raise money for the less fortunate, those needing extra support with medical expenses or other emergencies. After a time of chill conversation, my friend's cousin, Joey, nodded to me that he was heading back across the crowded room to the bathroom. I followed him, since I had to use it as well.

As we left the restrooms, a man confronted Joey (I'll call him Grumpy). None of us had seen him before. I couldn't hear everything being said but I understood from the body language that trouble was brewing. I pushed past others to be up close where I could hear. It was obvious that this dude was harassing Joey. It turned out, Grumpy had recently come from LA and was falsely accusing Joey of representing his old enemy gang. Something needed to be done before the conflict became physical. The two of them were beginning to square off and voices had lost all warmth. I confidently, yet diplomatically, placed myself in the eye of the storm.

With a feeble half grin, I put a gentle hand out toward both of them, "Hey, chavos, this town ain't big enough for this kind of mess. Here we all have to work together, this ain't LA," I said in my best street Spanish. "Forget that stuff man, ok. Aqui, estamos juntos"

Though he wasn't buying it 100%, Grumpy backed down, mumbled a few seemingly good-natured comments, and disappeared into the crowd. Joey and I returned to the table where we found another round of beers awaiting us. We talked and laughed some more and thought no more of the angry dude with a grudge. As the night wore on the lines between friendship and family began to fade. It was looking like a good night.

That was all about to change. A bit later Andre and one of his cousins went outside for some fresh air, and probably a smoke. Seizing on the break, I took the time to head towards the bathroom. Once inside, I saw Joey standing by the sinks, talking on the phone with his back to the wall, I nodded to him. As I turned, Grumpy came striding in.

It wasn't quite like a charge; we would have seen that coming. His entrance was more of an intentional strut. It appeared as though he was going to say something to Joey. However, instead of opening his mouth, he quickly extended his left fist from his side and smacked Joey in the cheek.

Joey's phone and beer went flying from the impact. This is where my rapid-fire decisions began to have long lasting consequences. I don't know why I responded as I did. Had I been trained as a true gang member, my initiation beat-down would have prepared me to return the assault with overwhelming retribution. Maybe it was the teacher part of me that responded by looking for how to break-up the fight. I'm not sure how it happened, but I found myself again in the middle. Without really thinking through what I would do next, I pushed the initial assailant back, yet my presence also prevented Joey from returning punches.

I was prepared to fight if Grumpy tried to land another punch on Joey. I would not hold back. To me "turning the other cheek" is giving people a second, or even a third chance, but it is not allowing people to just use you as a punching bag. (Remember, Jesus also used physical force to defend the exploited; don't forget that whooping with a whip in the temple!)

Rapidly, other onlookers gathered around and Grumpy retreated a step or two. Almost immediately, three or four of Grumpy's friends burst in the door. It was obvious they had planned their delayed entrance, expecting a fight to be underway, they would finish off what their friend had begun. Except there was no fight, they glanced around with disappointment clearly written on their faces. Just a few seconds behind them, the security guard came in and ordered everyone else out. I turned to Joey; his face covered in blood, yet what was even more disturbing was the rage that consumed his gaze.

As Joey attempted to stop his bleeding nose, the ivory sink slowly morphed into a crimson pool. The rage that had masked his face was now coupled by a completely separate emotion focused at me, deep disappointment. "Damn, man, why'd you do that?" His eyes began to tear up as his sense of shame swelled. He answered my look of disbelief with, "¿Que te pinche pienses? You held me back. You didn't even try to light him up."

Unable to reply, I stared at the bloody sink; I knew this would not be easily forgotten. Andre, Joey and their cousins are good men, men of their word and solid friends. They had been trained to live a code. "Sangre por sangre" - blood for blood. The bright crimson blood seemed almost florescent against the white ceramic sink basin. Soon more security returned, "You all need to leave, now!"

As we left the bathroom, the whole family met us. On one side were the cousins, angry and ready to exact retribution, on the other side was the great aunt. Tia looked at me and firmly said, "Take him home, straight home, and do NOT go looking for those guys." The cousins gave me the look that said, "Forget that, there's a debt of blood to be paid."

I took the keys and walked to the car. Tia shouted her commands once again. I did not, at that moment, know what I should do, what I would do, or even what I wanted to do. My thoughts were clouded by anger. For no good reason, some punk had smacked my friend and now he was in real pain. I wanted to get revenge, yet more than that I wanted to be respected by these friends.

We could drive the town looking for our fight. Someone mentioned we should get a gun, perhaps call another cousin who had access to a firearm. I then knew what I had to do. The words of Martin Luther King quietly stirred in my heart, "violence begets more violence." I knew peace had won in round one and two, and hate could not have a chance to even the score.

We got in the van, somebody shouted, "Let's go get 'em!" I took a deep breath, and clearly yet forcefully said, "No, man! We're going to the apartment. Tonight NO ONE is going to jail and NO ONE is going to get hurt or die."

For the next several hours I wrestled with what had happened that night. I vacillated between shame and security. When we got back to the apartment, Joey refused to look at me or talk to me. His anger and frustration deeply strained our friendship.

Andre confronted me, "Why did you let that happen? If I had been there…" I cut him off, "Well, you weren't – and it might be good you weren't. Look, we are all home and we are all safe." Andre glared at me and snapped back, "You let him get hit and didn't do shit!"

"I did NOT let them hit him," I retorted, "I was ready to fight if he tried to hit Joey again. But, think! If I had jumped on him… Man, when his boys rushed the bathroom, who knows what could have happened? At the very least we would have had a huge brawl. Who knows, they could have been packing blades or even more! The cops would have come, we all would have gotten arrested – and somebody could have gotten deported as well." I paused, "Look we are all here and we're ok."

Eventually Andre began to accept my actions. Later that night we drove back to Minneapolis. In my mind and spirit I wrestled with what had happened, "Did I do right or was I a coward who betrayed my friend out of fear for myself?"

The next morning we went to church, it was communion Sunday. I went forward and the usher extended to me the bread and then the cup. As I went to dip my bread in the cup I heard the words. "The blood of Jesus, that takes away the sins of the world." I was shocked as those words immediately brought to mind a bloody sink.

The blood of Jesus. The blood of Joey. The two images were in stark juxtaposition in my mind. As I looked into the cup questions flooded my mind. "Can the blood of Jesus really take away the sin of a bloodied nose? Can the blood of Jesus satisfy the thirst for revenge and mend bruised egos over gang grudges and pride?" Is this the supreme example of "sangre por sangre?"

As a bearer of Jesus' blood, we are sent to stand in the midst of pain and conflict as an empowered ambassador of peace. Being at that fiesta and in that bathroom gave me the sacred responsibility to be a peacemaker.

Blessed are the peacemakers, they will be called the children of God.

Consider...

Have you ever sensed the tension between being present and protecting your reputation?

How do you manage the tensions that arise between commitments to friends and personal values? Do they ever compete in your life?

Is there a difference between a peacemaker and a pacifist?

What do you think about Marque's interpretation of "...turning the other cheek?"

What is the role of a peacemaker in world of violence?

What is uncomfortable for you about this story?

Drivin' today from my 'hood to the other

Reflectin' on a memorial - for a slain brother

At a school, - where just 7 days before -

He completed high school

expecting much more!

In my 'hood, the grief is thick -

I wonder, in the other, do they even give a lick?

I'm not tryin' to start somethin' - I know some do care

But considerin' the reactions - Are folks even aware?

In my 'hood, the fear is real –

I wonder, in the other, do they even feel?

In up, and downtown - two white brothers die -

A Tragedy. - It captures the whole public eye…

But let a black or brown brother - Die in my 'hood -

Life goes on in the other - as if – "alls good!"

In my hood, boys and girls, also dream dreams

I wonder, in the other, can they even hear the screams?

Dedicated to the memory BC

A good kid, "in the wrong place at the wrong time"

"Accidental" victim of drive-by shooting

June 17, 2006

Real Peace: What Will it Take?

It all started when Donna stopped to talk; now after tragic news, a peace rally, and a phone call – I can't sleep. I was just walking out to my car when Donna pulled up with her daughter, and all the nieces and cousins in the back. She slowed to a roll when she saw me, "I just can't believe Frankie got killed." My puzzled look told her I had not yet put all the pieces together. "Frankie, Walter's brother, used to live around the corner. He was one of the dudes killed in the Steak House last week." The limited color drained completely from my face. I had heard the news, but I never put it together. 'Frank Eugene Haynes,' the name all over the news, was my old neighbor boy, Frankie.

Frankie had been Donna's neighbor too, back when they all lived on 17th. My sons, Jared and Tyler, were just little boys, and they looked up to Frankie and Lloyd. To my sons, they were older and wiser. They biked together, built forts together, and ruled Irving Avenue together.

With our little church, Frankie and the rest of the kids on our block went camping and did dozens of other little trips that opened them up to the world beyond North Minneapolis. Eventually, the worst of North Minneapolis would close in on Frank Haynes.

03.05.05 would be his last day on the North side. The pesky, energetic neighbor boy, now 21 years old, never finished his steak that day. Later, investigations proved that he was not even the intended target, but what difference does that make now? He's dead.

Donna told me that at the funeral, Walter, his "little" brother kept coming over to give her a hug. She also said that Frank had written a letter from jail, just a week before, saying that he knew he needed to get his life together and knew he needed Jesus to do it.

So that was just part one of a long evening. Later that night, I sat in the dark and wrote. I relived trips with Frankie, Walter, and Lloyd. But I also was confronted with a new face; Andrew.

I met Andrew that night at the peace walk. I mean, he didn't know he was gong to a peace walk. He just went to the corner of Irving and 26th to do his typical Friday night job; sell drugs. The peace walk came to him.

A thousand or more people lined 26th Ave. along the North side for 16 blocks. I'm sure we were an annoyance to Andrew and his boys. It had to hamper the willingness of suburban and urban clients that drove into my community to visit the open market of illegal substances. But they had to wait us out; we would leave shortly after dark and they would continue to rule "their" turf.

Several from the "Peace Walk" had crossed the street to approach this group of "black males in their late teens to early twenties." (Bet you haven't heard that phrase before). A young woman with her baby was one of several who went to give a flyer and invitation to the Peace Walk and the party that was to follow. They were polite, but short, with these distractions, impatient to reclaim "their" open marketplace.

I left the crowd to get something from my van, as I returned I intentionally walked back on "their" side of the street. Up ahead of me, I watched as a local resident leader stopped to talk to the group. They had seen him before. He's a good guy, but from the perspective of these fellas, his agenda was to get THEM out of HIS turf. I watched from about half a block a way as he encouraged them to "…come join the festivities for peace."

As I approached I heard someone from the back of the group exclaim, "FUCK PEACE!" By this time, I was on the block and the good hearted man with the invitation was on his way to something more hospitable. Two young men were in lawn chairs near the sidewalk, the rest were gathered in the lawn and on the front steps. As I passed, I gave the urban-polite nod and perfunctory "what's-up!" Several answered with various affirming responses. I kept walking, but every step grew heavier, until I knew I needed to return. Andrew said later he knew it was God that turned me around.

I came back angered that one of these thugs could be so calloused as to say, "F- peace!" I was still grieving the news that one of my kids from years past was gunned down by such a callous spirit. I came back because I knew these "gangsters" were just boys trying to make a broken life work. I came back because I knew they saw US as their enemy, wanting their turf; not their best interests.

I stepped in front of the guys in the lawn chairs and calmly addressed the group. "Did one of ya'all just say 'fuck peace?'" Several denials came quickly, as did a small crowd.

Several guys stepped aggressively closer and I realized that I hadn't planned my next line; thankfully someone else had. "Look, I don't have nothin' but love for all y'all," some positive nods and gestures let me know that this was going in the right direction. "We're just out here to let y'all know you don't have to be out here selling and bangin' to make it."

This is where Andrew interrupted me. "Man, I know I'm out here doing illegal shit. If I had a job I wouldn't need to be here." I looked hard at him; I was quite sure he was telling the truth. But was he also calling my bluff? Could I, can we, offer him anything but a thousand people interrupting his business?

I took a leap of faith. "Look, bro, if you're serious, I'll give you my number. Call me. I've got connections and we can get you a job." He pulled out his cell and entered in my number and name. "This is your direct number?" he inquired. I pulled my phone from my pocket, "If you punch it in, this'll ring right now."

I asked him, "How old are you, man?" "Seventeen." I looked at him and the other young men who had now gathered around us. The mood had completely changed. "Ya know, I've lived in this neighborhood since you were a baby, and I've seen way too many funerals for young brothers. I don't want to have to go to anymore this summer. Y'all take it easy out here." As I turned to go, Andrew and the crew gave me the proper farewells. "Hey, man I'll maybe hit you off later!" I headed back to the crowd and thought, "Yeah sure, he might call, but I won't hold my breath."

Before 10pm, my phone rang. "Hey, what's–up? This is Andrew." He quickly told me several defining things, including how the night before, he had been on his knees crying out to God for a way out of the streets. He thought he could trust me because of the way I came to him and his boys. He had a baby on the way and wanted to do the right thing.

I told him I would start calling my contacts looking for a job. We made plans for church on Sunday and hanging-out with some good men on Saturday. We both agreed; God had turned me around to go back and talk.

I don't wonder why I went back. I do wonder, when will the church and all the "Peace Walkers" wake up from their dreams of simple solutions to the complex craziness of the streets? Will we wake from our slumber and put action to our words. Are we willing to face sacrifice, and really do something to help this brother get off the street? If we would, we could easily become a community that will provide enough referrals and mentors to help brothers like Andrew succeed.

Will we help him, and so many others, see Jesus? Not as a mantra we recite for security, but as the man we follow to the cross.

Consider...

From what seeds does violence grow?

How do you usually respond when someone uses profanity in connection with a serious issue?

How do you feel about using profanity to drive home a point?

What most strikes you about this story?

I often see people on the streets doing "outreach" for a night, but seldom reaching out to build friendships over time. What problems does this approach cause?

What would you say are keys to building "real peace" and not just doing peace events?

Street-wize Eyez

Street-wize eyez see the street,

From their space on the street

Where concrete and blood often meet

And life – death ; joy and pain

In the hustle compete.

These eyes seldom meet

Those in the drivers seat

Driver's-seat-eyez roll by with comforts complete

And fear to look into the street-wize eyes

Windows – up, AC on, radio to fill the silent space

Drivers – side - eyes flick the lock and dare not see the face from that other space

To connect with street-wize eyez – risks an un-welcomed embrace

You KNOW –

The homeless vet – wants yo dolla' –

that hooka — jus' wants to holla'

And the dude @ the corner – where no bus stops –

He's just runnin shop

With a dime bag or a hunk of dat rock

YOU KNOW –

YOU KNOW???

Cuz… – you watch the news?

Cuz – they once sang you the blues?

Or - cuz you got a short racist fuse?

- maybe?? Or jus maybe…

—— cuz you don't wanna remember

U was once in dem shoes –

Or perhaps you jus' believe -

they choose to lose!

Now don't get me twisted, it's not a

black and white game.

Black – white or brown – they'll roll by,

jus the same…

Unwilling to look U in the eyes

out of fear or shame.

Street-wize eyez also - come in all colors

out here - they all brothers

Back to the wall – tryin' to stay tall

United in the hustle – yet fightin' not to fall!

So street-wize eyez seek to survive

And drivers side eyes jus wanna get by

Protected – unaffected –

never mindin' if those on the curb are rejected

We in Separate worlds!

Our eyez don't meet when our paths do cross.

What is the cost of the cross?

And IF...

If eyes should lock – by chance or by destiny

I wonder would we see humanity?

or even ——- divinity?

Dakota Journey

It was a cold clear December afternoon and the sun was quickly approaching the treeless horizon on the Minnesota prairie. I leaned into Austin, the energetic Arabian Quarter horse I had been riding the past few days, both for warmth and to maintain our united rhythm. We were into the second week of the ride and so the initial ache in my legs and behind was subsiding. I began to adapt to the repetitive motion needed to keep me moving smoothly with the constant trotting of my horse. I had ridden before, but this was totally different, both in pace and purpose. Never had I ridden at such a sustained rapid pace for so long. It was not a pleasure ride, nor a work activity; we were participants in a Dakota Ceremony, accompanying the sacred staff with 40 eagle feathers.

I was riding with descendants of the Dakota who had been banished from Minnesota following the brief war of 1862. Each of them had stories of ancestors who were directly impacted by that event. Some of the relatives met the gallows in Mankato while others were spared immediate death to spend years in prison. Others knew the stories of family who had survived the forced marches, internment camps, barges and cattle cars. I felt greatly honored and slightly out of place. I knew my presence was welcomed even ordained by the Creator, yet my mind and emotions struggled to comprehend the purpose and importance of this 14 day event.

As we rode this evening, my mind was drawn to the fact that we were now on land that had felt the direct blow of the anger and pain that overflowed when years of injustice from state agents and traders was left unchecked. The conflict erupted when the very survival of the Dakota was in question.

I could envision the landscape one hundred and fifty years ago; this same prairie, just fewer communities, no major roads and only the scattered homes of settlers. The conflict that broke-out between the Dakota who were facing starvation, and the settlers who were arriving weekly in new waves, would dramatically alter the future of the state of Minnesota as well as the relationship between the Native People of this land and the United States Government. The events of time gone by have left a lasting scar on our physical and social community. Yet now, I was a part of a ceremony of remembrance, healing and reconciliation.

My participation in the ride was only the logical progression of a journey that had been initiated several years ago as I began to learn about the Dakota/Minnesota war of 1862. For my teaching and preaching, I was searching for examples of racism and injustice that were closer to home for us in Minnesota than the issues of slavery and segregation. Many northerners I encounter feel that those issues are far away and thus prove that we in the North are free from any race-based guilt. I didn't have to look far.

I first discovered a 20th Century lynching in Duluth and then learned about this war that had grown from intentional racial injuries and resulted in our own Minnesota-version of the "Trail of Tears" and ethnic cleansing. However, few Minnesotans are aware that this shameful event played an essential role in molding the identity of the state we know today.

This journey of discovery led my wife and I to Mankato on December 2010 to participate in the annual remembrance of the largest mass execution in US history. On the day after Christmas, 1862, thirty-eight Dakota warriors were hung before hundreds of angry settlers for their role in the 6 week war. The state leaders of Minnesota had wanted to execute over 300 Dakota men, however President Lincoln reduced the number to 38. Lincoln was troubled by the speed of the trials and the lack of evidence against the accused, it seems he to some extent agreed with the argument of Bishop Whipple who wrote in September of 1862; *"Who is guilty of the causes which desolated our border? At whose door is the blood of these innocent victims? I believe that God will hold the nation (USA) guilty"* (*Lights and Shadows of a Long Episcopate, p 435*)

However the white invaders had be stung deeply by the brutal attacks on their towns and homes, and now few cared if innocent Dakota were killed. Most of these new immigrants did not want justice, they wanted revenge. Lincoln may have saved some from execution, but Minnesota was not satisfied with anything less than the complete removal of the Dakota, and all other tribes, from southern MN. As a result the treaties were cancelled, reservation lands were seized, and all Dakota were forcibly resettled to a prison camp at Fort Thompson (the Crow Creek reservation).

This ethnic cleansing was mandated regardless of a tribe's involvement in the war. The truth is most Dakota groups did NOT participate in hostilities and many were active in protecting and helping settlers. Most Dakota were marched to Fort Snelling to endure the winter in an internment camp. In the spring they were loaded on barges and shipped like cattle to Fort Thompson, a military outpost, along the Missouri river in East Central South Dakota. Additionally, others fled into Canada where their descendants live today with unclear refugee status. At that time Minnesota offered bounty hunters up to $200 (in 1863 dollars!) for the scalp of a Dakota found in the State.

And so I met Peter Lengkeek while in Mankato with Janeen. I first saw him at the Memorial Site sitting high on his horse, holding the staff with the 40 eagle feathers (to represent the 38 who had been executed in that very place and the 2 additional Dakota who were later executed outside of Fort Snelling in Minneapolis.) His words were reverant as he recalled the events of 1862 and explained the purpose of the journey they had just made from Crow Creek to Mankato over the past 16 days. Peter is a Crow Creek tribal leader and was the staff-bearer for that Dakota 38 memorial ride. He is a person who quietly invokes respect. He is tall and thin, when he speaks his words are intentional, quiet and yet powerful. However he did not only speak of the painful past, Peter spoke of a hopeful future of forgiveness and reconciliation.

After the memorial service there was a feast, created by the food brought by guests and ride participants. Janeen and I helped to serve. Before we left, I knew I had to meet this man whose presence and words demanded my respect. Little did I know this meeting was the start of a journey to deeper awareness, respect, and connection with my Dakota brothers.

That December meeting with Peter opened the doors for me to share the sacred story of the 38 alongside Dakota and Lakota leaders in various settings across the Twin Cities. These events, in turn led to my involvement in the Dakota 38+2 ride of 2012. The two weeks I spent with these amazing men, women, and horses has had a profound impact on my life. Yet I cannot now give a definitive account of what has happened through that journey, in part because so much of the story is still being written. The following are the posts and letters I wrote during and after that ride with a few revisions and clarifications.

Consider...

Have you had experiences that opened doors and drew you into a new community?

What are the "guides" or limitations that determine if you peruse an opportunity to venture beyond your normal cultural experiences?

What has been your experiences with and awareness of Native American individuals and communities?

If you are Native American, how does that part of your identity impacted your daily life?

On the Road to Crow Creek

9DEC

As the snow was swirling around our garage, I loaded up my bags filled with winter wear as well as the saddle and bridles I had brought for the ride. Peter let me know that while they had plenty of horses they could always use more tack to assure everyone had the equipment to ride.

Janeen drove me to meet Keith, another ride participant who was on his way from Wisconsin with a load of hay. He met me on the exit of Pioneer Trail. I was stuck by a strange sense of irony that my journey was beginning at place named not for those who made the trail (the Dakota who had lived along the Minnesota River for Centuries), but those who had taken possession of it, the Pioneers. We made our way through the snow, down Highway169 to St. Peter and then headed into the section of the Minnesota River Valley where 150 years ago this war had been waged.

We got to Courtland and found the pasture where we were to leave the hay for the horses that will be riding into this town later next week. A plaque in the town center simply states *"1862 – 9 people were murdered in the Sioux Uprising"* As we left for Morton the snow was diminishing and the roads were clear. We expected that we would be in Fort Thompson by midnight. As we drove, Keith and I had an enjoyable time exchanging stories of life.

As we got closer to Morton the weather took a turn, colder winds converted the light mist into a driving snow. This area had much more snow on the ground and the winds were now driving it into drifts. We met Darwin Strong, one of the ride coordinators, at the gas station / hotel, he wondered how we had gotten this far. We followed him to his farm, which shares a driveway with the Birch Coulee battle site. The road, the ditches, and the sky were all various hues of white making our drive slow and treacherous.

At his farm we loaded up 1,000 lbs of Purina Horse Feed. The feed was donated to the ride after a Land-o-Lakes employee watched the Dakota 38 movie at Bethel University. The employee noticed a farmer in the documentary wearing a Purina jacket, so they made some connections and a donation of 140 bags of much needed horse feed was made.

The sun was setting somewhere behind the blowing snow; and spurred by Darwin's advice, we decided to stay at the hotel connected to the gas station. Hopefully the snow and wind would let up and we could head out early the next day to meet up with the other riders at Lower Brule and Crow Creek.

That night we slept in peace in the midst of what 150 years ago had been ground zero in the Dakota / MN war of 1862.

Sunset Over Crow Creek

10DEC

We made it onto the Crow Creek Reservation right as the riders were making their way from the Lower Brule reservation by crossing the Missouri River. Here the road runs atop of the *Big Bend Dam*, a huge earthen wall that stops-up the river and generates electricity for much of South Dakota and the region. A lovely lake was created, but came at a huge cost to the Indian Reservations along the river in the 1950s and 1960s. When the Army Corp came in to flood the river, the tribes on both sides (Lower Brule and Crow Creek) were again forced to relocate; this time from the fertile banks of the river, to the more desolate, unprotected bluffs.

Once we got to Fort Thompson, we connected with Peter and met other riders over dinner in the community center. I then joined a group going out to feed and water the horses which were kept in a corral on the edge of town. Later, we met up with a group in the hotel lobby and participated in a sweat lodge.

I have a million thoughts now as I wrote, was thankful to be there, and I greatly anticipated what our Creator would do with this time and place.

Consider...

How do you feel / react when you are in a new environment or situation?

How do you see / feel personal ties to historical events?

Are you ever aware of history in places you live/visit, how have you seen the role that history has on the present?

As Day Comes to a Close Over the SD Plains: New Insights and Friendships Emerge

11DEC

I sit on my bed now contemplating the day past. As I consider the words spoken and the deeds done, I am aware of how little I know and how little I am. Yet, I am encouraged at how big God is and how good God's people are.

A few days ago I had a dream, in this dream I didn't ride at all, but I worked in support and drove trucks. This is also what some of my mentors suggested should be my posture, to be present and to assist as I can. I realize I am here to help, and to ride is an honor so great I will not invite myself to partake in it. Today was a day of walking, working, listening and learning!

The day began with rounding up the horses from the corral and loading them on trailers. We drove to the ceremony site on the dam, the same place where the riders had concluded the day before. The morning sun was bright, the air was crisp, and the view across the river valley and the vast prairie was breath-taking.

As we unloaded the horses I sought to find my role in saddling, feeding, and generally supporting the riders; I began with the limited relationships I had made in the past 16 hours. We had briefly met a few people at the Sweat Lodge, and at breakfast that morning, but my circle of connection was still mainly Keith, who had given me a ride from Minneapolis, and Healer, who shared his room with us the night before.

At breakfast, while sipping on coffee and eating my eggs, pancakes and sausage I noticed that we were the only three white guys and I wondered, "Why were all the white boys sitting together in the cafeteria...?" I realized that unless I intentionally break out of this web, of similar looking, good intentioned men, I believe I will be labeled and grouped with them for the entire trip. As good as these guys are, I do not want to live in the confines of these limiting constructs.

Gradually the horses are unloaded from the trailers, curried, bridled, and saddled. I offer to help as I can, my help is welcome but conversations are limited. It seems that each trailer load represents families or groups, many from other Dakota reservations. School buses arrived with the middle and high school students from Crow Creek. Eventually the horses, students, guests and participants circle up for the ceremony.

We are atop an earthen structure that did not exist 150 years ago but we are near the place where those barges made their landing in the late summer of 1863, the original Fort Thompson. It was here that the Dakota, who were now exiles and prisoners of war, were forced to unload and try to eke out a living amid extremely harsh conditions. Peter recounted some of those realities: Mothers searching through the dung of the horses of the US Cavalry to find corn to feed their children, warriors unable to leave the small compound to hunt for food while their families were facing starvation, women selling their most important possession to unappreciative soldiers to get food for themselves and their loved ones. We shared in a purification ceremony, various songs and prayers were spoken. The riders circled several times and then rode off towards Mankato following the Staff of the 38 + 2.

There were way more participants today than horses, as the riders headed up the road the students loaded buses which proclaimed "CROW CREEK CHEIFTANS." Everyone else got into their cars and trucks to follow the riders with a respect that was both somber and yet exuberant and proud.

Keith and Healer invited me to jump in the truck, but I had already determined that I could not allow this sacred moment to be severed from the earth on which I stood by riding in a vehicle where I know my thoughts would also be disturbed by the conversation of others. I wanted to walk, I had to walk, to reflect on the opening ceremony and this tragic history; yet also to consider the stunning bravery, that occurred in *this* place. Many times in the last 2 days have I heard of the courage and strength of the Dakota people who survived the horrific conditions they faced when deposited in this place. The men, women and children I am with all trace their family through this time, place and events. I am a humbled to be walking on the same ground as such great people.

I spent most of the morning walking behind the horses and alongside the row of trailers that followed. Several people offered me a ride, but most understood the concept of needing and wanting to walk. Later, I rode more, especially as the pace picked up once we left the broad valley of Fort Thompson and the Missouri River. It was then I began to make additional acquaintances.

After lunch Peter shared that we had been offered the opportunity to corral the horses with a rancher a few miles past the border of the reservation. Some of the young men on the ride work for him and as he learned about the ride he became willing to help out. In past years, the horses were loaded on trailers and returned to Crow Creek for the night and then trailered back to resume the ride the next day. This gesture of hospitality and kindness would save money and time. However, he did not have the corral prepared, so people needed to come to the ranch to set-up the corral panels and get the pens ready for the horses. The young men who worked for the rancher were going. A few others, Keith, Healer and I also volunteered.

At the ranch, the snow was deep and it was not easy to move the panel sections to set-up the corral but it was rewarding work and good time to get to know other riders as well. The rancher also provided plenty of hay and lots of fresh water for the weary horses. After all the horses were running free in the corral we loaded up and headed back to Fort Thompson for dinner and rest in the hotel.

After eating dinner together in the Crow Creek community center, Peter Lengkeek shared how thankful he is for the group and the opportunity again to ride. He went on to say, "I want you to be aware of something. Tomorrow we will ride though the town of

Wessington Springs." Peter explained that we are going to be hosted to lunch at the Legion Hall by several families who want to welcome and support the Dakota 38 ride. "We are very thankful for their hospitality," he said, "however, it is important to know that many of the first citizens of this town were bounty hunters, who came to track down and kill our people as they fled MN." Bounty hunters were paid $25 – $200 for the scalp of a Dakota if they were caught "off the reservation." Suddenly a term that I had often heard thrown around loosely was given a meaning I had never fully considered.

Peter went on to say that in the 1970s, two white men drove to Crow Creek with several boxes. The men were the schools' principals. In the boxes were bones of Dakota men and women who had been killed by the bounty hunters. Up until that time the bones had been *displayed in the school*. Dakota spiritual leaders took the bones and gave them a proper burial. Peter shared that while things are changing in Wessington Springs, the history of hostility has not completely ended.

Just a short time ago a basketball game had an ugly aftermath. The Crow Creek Chieftains had badly defeated the Wessington Springs Spartans and a mob of angry students and fans cornered and intimidated the Crow Creek students who were gripped with fear.

Peter concluded his talk by saying, "There are many good people in this town, yet there are still some who hate us. So tonight as you go to bed, tomorrow when you wake, pray for those people who hate. Pray for them that one day we may be able to walk side by side as brothers on this earth."

This is the call of love, forgiveness and reconciliation. I heard Peter's words echoing the words of Christ "Love your enemies and pray for those who persecute you" Matthew 5:44.

There is much to learn so that we can walk side-by-side in peace.

Consider...

Have you ever had an experience like the one Marque described in which you had to break out of the prescribed roles to have time and space to reflect? At times is that need connected to the place you are at? How/why?

Are you aware of how the perceptions of others may stereotype you, because of who you are and with whom you associate? When / Where? Is it right to intentionally work to break out of the roles others may naturally try to put you into?

Have there been times when you were unsure of the role you could/should have in an event? Is participation usually a right or a privilege?

How does Peter's story of the bounty hunters of the past and the need to pray today connect with situations you too have faced?

Sunset Over Woonsocket SD

12DEC

Today I was invited by Richard to ride his horse, Austin. Richard was one of the men who helped to prepare the panels for the corral the day before. He told me straight-up that Austin is a spirited horse and the same one that Healer had fallen from the year before when he let him get running too fast. I assured him I could keep him reigned in, but he also let me know I'd been warned.

After we saddled up the horses I rode him around a bit to warm-up. Several people helped me get my stirrups adjusted right (only later did I really understand the importance on such a ride). One of the other riders, Jake, who I had met in Minneapolis last year while showing the Dakota 38 documentary with his Uncle Jim Miller, insisted that I trade my Timberland boots for his sleeker cowboy boots so that my foot would be less likely to get caught in the stirrup should I fall. I was grateful and yet somewhat self-conscious for all the attention I was receiving. As I rode around the yard, I felt confident with the horse but, yet again, unworthy to have a place in a saddle so early on the ride. However I was honored Richard believed he could trust me with his brother, this glorious horse, Austin.

It was a great day to ride, clear skies, warm December weather but most significant was the company in which I road. For a while a young girl rode behind me on Austin after Richard suggested he would be a great horse for riding double. Her mother was looking for a place for her so she could experience the ride. She was great company and talked with me, her brother, and the young men from Crow Creek. The lunch stop in Wessington Springs went well. Fresh water for the horses, good sandwiches for the riders, but having heard Peter's story from the night before it made you wonder what was behind the glances we received from the towns people. Yet as we heard, the offer to stop and the presence of people willing to host lunch are a welcomed sign of change; reconciliation and healing taking place.

Richard and I would rotate between riding Austin, his other horse Dash, or driving along in the truck. That evening I was able to accompany the staff into town after we pushed the last 5 miles into Woonsocket. My legs are killing me. My butt is so sore. I have never ridden *so* fast for *so* long and I need to better learn to work with the stirrups. Some of the guys were making fun of me "making pancakes" as my butt slapped against the saddle.

This is where we will eat dinner and sleep in the community center. I'm not physically as sore as I feared, but at times my raw emotions do flare up. Between feelings of unjustified honor and welcome and then overwhelming and well-deserved shame and sorrow. My thoughts jar from place to place and even as I try to find a smoother rhythm in the saddle and with my horse, I pray my soul will find rhythm between the competing emotions that pull me from side to side.

I feel unable to identify, much less verbalize all my feelings and thoughts, someday this experience will find words and someday these seeds being planted will take root and bear fruit. However I believe, we must be willing to do the hard work forgiveness and reconciliation demand. We must allow the fruit we hold tightly to be used as seed so future generations can eat something besides bitter grapes.

Consider...

What is the fruit you hold tightly?

What are the bitter grapes our society consumes?

How can that fruit you hold become seeds for the good fruit of future generations?

Have you ever felt self-conscious yet honored by the attention you received in cross-cultural experiences?

Riding to Howard SD, Following the Ancient Dakota Highway.

13DEC

"Wasicu" the Dakota word literally means *one-who-takes-the-fat*. (Wasi=fat, Cu=one who takes) Peter explained to me that first contact between the Europeans and Dakota occurred at a time when the white explorers/trappers were starving. The hungry invaders would sneak into Dakota camps and cut off fat from the drying buffalo meat. Many people today only know "wasicu" as the word for white-man, few know the etymology. However the word became more than appropriate as the immigrant hoards again and again took the "fat" of the land.

The road we have been traveling, SD Highway 34, was an ancient passageway from Minnesota, across the Missouri River, and into the Black Hills. It was frequently traveled by Lakota, Nakota, and Dakota bands. Now we travel the road east from what became a prison camp and later the reservation to where most of the Dakota were banished after the war of 1862. Many of the riders from Crow Creek have relatives who tried to get back to MN after the prison-camp era ended. They too, followed this trail while trying to escape bounty hunters. As we rode Peter encouraged us to think of those relatives who traveled this route.

Today, to ride as fast a possible, we ran relays. With 40 miles to cover, a fresh group of 4-8 would head out for a hard 5 miles, there another group would take the staff and launch out for the next 5 miles.

As I've had the honor to be one of the riders following the staff with 40 eagle feathers, I ponder the significance. Riding with those whose ancestors were hung, exiled, hunted, and hated, while my ancestors received the "Wasi" of the land. Almost all of my eight great-grandparents were the settlers who moved into Iowa and Nebraska immediately after the Native people were forcefully removed, and in ways not all that different from the Minnesota story.

As I shared with one of my new friends today; "if we can ride in peace together now, while also symbolically and spiritually riding for our ancestors, perhaps healing can begin from wounds inflicted long ago."

Consider...

Who were your ancestors? What roles did they play in American history? How did their experiences trickle down into your life?

Can pain of the past be undone? If so, how? If not, why?

Letter emailed

17DEC

After the first week out we were at a hotel and I took the chance to write an email to the small group of people who had donated funds which allowed me to leave my job and still pay bills at home. This is bulk of that letter which explains some of the deeper feelings and emotions I was experiencing at this time:

Dear Friends,

Sunday night sitting in my room, wondering what is happening and how to put it into words.

First of all, I want to send thanks to each of you who made it possible to leave home and family for two weeks to be part of this amazing experience. Hopefully you've been able to follow some of the blog posts I've written at mmjmpls.com but what I want to share with you is more intimate and personal than what I can share in a blog.

FIRST - this has been an exercise in cross-cultural communication like *nothing* I've done before.

I don't know If you were like me in junior high (I hope not), but I was a hot mess, trying to find my way socially - wanting to make friends, but not quite knowing the rules I was supposed to follow. There was this "feeling" that you are awkward and inappropriate. While the motivation and ability to process this has changed in the last 35+ years the same feelings have been experienced in the past week.

- Was I just slighted because I did something really stupid, or was I not slighted at all?

- Is that a joke that I should laugh at, or was that a serious statement?

- I know THAT was a joke, everybody is laughing, but *what* was the punch-line?

Yea, this is a new culture, even language and hand signals that I don't understand and yet people have been patient and welcoming on every turn. I am in awe that this beautiful culture is so unknown to most Americans, yet it is one of the original cultures of America.

An example of cultural norms and expectations: The people I did know coming in, never gave me a "pass" or an introduction to the group. I guess I expected a little of that "connection-power" that is common with white-American culture. For example, Peter could have said "this is Marque he is my friend," and in essence said I am "safe" " Instead he has forced me (and the other non Natives) to stand on our own 2 feet. We had to earn respect naturally and work through our struggle to understand and connect. I've tried to live by a line I've often said - "Listen, Listen... Learn" it has been tough, but as a result some people here really think that I'm a quiet person...???? lol

(In retrospect I am SO thankful I did not get an introduction or a "pass." First of all, it would not have been culturally appropriate, and secondly, I am a better man because of the struggle I had to make to meet people and be myself.)

SECOND - I've learned *"You don't know a fuckin' thing, whitey"* - that was said to me "in *love*" by the guy who first let me ride his horse, lets me drive his truck, and who has been painfully honest with me at every turn, He was explaining to me how broken and twisted the reservation system is, at one point he was breaking down to me how "sovereign nations" are the most federally controlled places in the USA. Not knowing how to respond, I let a casual "I know" slip out of my mouth. (Just like white folks, we think we have to add to the silence a punctuation of our awareness) That's when he cut me off, with his blunt, yet true statement and I was reminded how stupid and privileged I am- all I could say is "Your right"

I am riding with men and women who are the descendants of those who were executed in Mankato, who were pardoned by Lincoln and then imprisoned in Davenport Iowa for years. A young man who rides often with me, (on horse and in the truck) is teaching me a TON, he is a direct descendant of Chief Big Foot, who fought with Sitting Bull at Little Bighorn in the defeat of General Custer, and was later massacred at Wounded Knee.

My friend, who reminded me of how little I know, shared how his dad HATED all white men, had been beaten up by them and fought them every chance he could. I can't understand this legacy, but I can learn to listen to those who have such a legacy and I am beginning to learn so much!

I realize how even my sense of geography is tied to my identity. I know places in the USA by what state they are in, however the people I am riding with again and again speak of the Reservations they are from and visit and have lived on, it seems the state has little or no significance. I never realized how many reservations there are, it often seems as if we view the US map almost in an opposite way. After asking a few times, "what state is that in?" "or where is that?" I realized I need to shut-up and go look at a map, learn something and stop asking stupid questions...

My blunt honest friend also is interested to talk with me about the Jesus I know, who is much *unlike* the Christ forced on him and his parents. . I'll again be driving his truck and riding his prized horses tomorrow as we joke and talk and maybe even bump into that strange beast of "Beloved Community"

THIRD - I have a lot to learn about love, prayer and forgiveness. Every morning we begin the day with a circle for prayers to the creator and we share in the Chanupa (pipe). We pray for strength, for families back home, and Peter always reminds us to pray for the people "that pass us, especially those who give us evil looks, pray for the towns we ride through and the homes we pass." He reminds us of the power of "praying for the people who might even hate us and what we are doing" Yet he sees the changing of attitudes and the new welcomes the riders find as proof that the Creator is using this ride as a way to heal and bring reconciliation.

An example, as soon as we learned of the shooting at the elementary school in Massachusetts, Peter called us to pray for the families affected and even the family of the shooter. At that time we were at Dakota State University and one woman from a local church that brought us food commented that she knew of no white groups that stopped for prayer immediately upon hearing the news. Peter stressed this is the way of the Dakota, Lakota, and Nakota people; Peace and unity of all...

Every day I feel more and more a part of the crew -everyday I learn more - and daily I am grateful to be here

Thanks for your part in helping me be here! (emotionally, spiritually, and financially)

Consider...

What aspect of this letter do you..

...most relate to?

..find most troubling?

...see as encouraging?

Have you ever had to really admit that you "...don't know anything?" Why is that difficult? In the long run is it humbling or empowering to take such a position?

Riding Together to Live Together

20DEC

Riding across the southwest MN plains it was not hard to picture what these rolling hills would have looked like 150 years ago. Remove the wind blocks and groves of trees, mentally photo-shop out the farms, railroad, and roads and I began to imagine what it may have looked like to have been riding with Little Crow and his men during the fall of 1862. It was not hard to picture as many of those riding with me are direct descendants of those who fought in this short but devastating war. Add to that the fact that the songs, prayers and ceremonies we share in each day have changed little since the 1860's.

By this date, December 20, 1862 - most of the MN Dakota had been arrested, many had been marched to Fort Snelling, while others were fleeing into Canada or further west. As we ride it is impossible not to ponder how this "Dakota38+2 Memorial Ride' honors those who rose up against a system and people. They rose up against those who were willing to allow them to starve while food was stored up within their grasp; because greedy traders and agents turned cold hearts to the suffering around them. Even President Lincoln, who signed the death orders for the 38, accepted the argument that the Dakota had a right to go to war, since they were a sovereign nation and the terms of a treaty had been violated putting their survival in jeopardy.

However, riding across the prairie I also had to consider the others whose lives were drastically impacted: the innocent settlers who had no direct role in to the violation of treaties. Yet they suffered destruction of property, death, and were held as hostages. I thought of them as well as we crossed the prairie. I could imagine the homes from which some had fled and others had been killed. Today in the distance I saw a rising cloud of smoke and I imagined the terror of having your farm and house burned while witnessing your unsuspecting friends and family members slaughtered. I also thought of the Minnesota Military who rode with Alexander Sibley,

I wondered what they felt perusing the Dakota warriors, and later as they were guarding the women and children and forcing them to march cross-country in the winter cold.

It would be much easier to talk and work for reconciliation if all injustice was one-directional, but it is always more complex. We must deal with the horrors settlers faced, while openly acknowledging the gross injustices inflicted on the Dakota. The raids on settlers did not occur in a vacuum, but by men backed into a corner who had tried to do all they could to live in peace with the white invaders. Yet, to most of the unsuspecting settlers, the attacks probably seemed unprovoked. To live in peace with all: that is the meaning of the name Dakota, yet they are a people who would fight to defend their families and way of life.

Besides historical and philosophical integrity I have an additional reason I must wrestle with the settler's side of the story; *the settler is my ancestor.* While my people were not here in Minnesota they were not unlike these immigrant settlers. My great-grandparents settled in Nebraska and Iowa, they were the sod-busters who took position of the land as soon as the Native people were forced off. Their heritage and perspective were similar to those in Minnesota and so I cannot believe that their views on the native people were much different.

Today as we spoke at the school in Russell, Peter Lengkeek, a direct descendant of these Dakota warriors acknowledged the terror that had been inflicted on settlers and said, "We want to be the first to say we are sorry, it is the only path to healing and reconciliation." One girl in the room knew that some of her ancestors had been killed during the war.

At the invitation of Richard I spoke as well. He asked that I shared my own ancestors' story. He and I had discussed these issues at length along the journey. I connected with many students as I told the story of my Danish ancestors who had settled the prairies that the Dakota and other Native Peoples had been forced to vacate. I tried to challenge the students to take responsibility to use the resources and opportunities they have been given, not just for self, but for others. I referred to Beverly Tatum's statement in "Race the Power of an Illusion" where she makes the point that while none of us asked to be born into the unjust systems around us we can all ask the question "What can I do?" to make the world around me more equitable for all.

So here I ride with descendants of the Dakota 38, new found friends and warriors for peace, their love and humility make me feel small in the presence of their greatness. They offer the white community a lesson in forgiveness and love. But if reconciliation that bears the fruit of justice is to occur, the message of these riders must be met with more than a smile and a wave. The riders are a great doorway through which all Americans may come to awareness and witness an example of love and humility. But true reconciliation requires that all resources are made available, including open minds, open hearts, and an openess to new economic practices. Then perhaps, we can together begin to create a new future where we openly acknowledge the sins of the past while working together to find pathways that undo the inequalities of today. Inequalities which are the result of the unjust policies which followed this little war and it's devastating and lasting impacts.

Consider...

Why do we tend to only want to view most scenarios of conflict from one vantage point? Is it important that Marque (and all of us) listen to the victims on all sides of a conflict?

What must accompany "smiles and waves" if true reconciliation is to occur?

What is your answer to the question Marque asked the students in Russell, What can I do, from my position and perspective to make the world around me a more equitable place for all?

Standing in Solidarity with the Dakota this December 26

22DEC

Consider doing something different on the day after Christmas, yet something so like what Jesus did. *Put yourself in an uncomfortable place for the sake of reconciliation.*

Let me explain.

A few days back I had participated in my second inipi (sweat lodge) since I joined with the Dakota 38 riders. With the exception of the external environment, I found it very similar to a intimate prayer gathering in the home of a friend. Trade the guitar for a drum, however the intent and the prayers are about the same. After the inipi ceremony we stood outside in the snow, preparing to go in for a meal. I was reflecting on the past days with the ride. I was overwhelmed by the welcome and love I was shown, these men and women could have so many reasons to hate me and what I culturally and socially represent, yet I have been given the honor to be called a brother. I was humbled, I could feel the love of God, the Creator, I could see the forgiveness and grace that Jesus demonstrated.

I began to think of where this ride was headed to; the hanging site in Mankato. The place where my new-found brother's direct ancestors had been killed after trials that lasted a few minutes. I know some Minnesotans say, "How can we honor the Dakota 38?" These riders themselves will be the first to tell you that, "Yes, there were horrific acts committed by some Dakota during that short war." They also declare, "we are here to step up and say we are sorry." However, many innocent Dakota men went to the gallows that day, and the horrors inflicted on women, children, even the Dakota who never took up arms, are indefensible. All of that tragedy, all the hate, and the generations of suffering that follow to this day, focus back on that moment. December 26, 1862, 10 am.

We are headed to Mankato to enter into that same place, at that same hour, 150 years later.

I know I would be welcomed by my Dakota sisters and brothers to ride with them into Mankato. However, I do not feel I am worthy, nor is it an honor I deserve. As I stood outside that inipi and envisioned the 26th, an image of what seemed appropriate began to appear in my mind. Yes, 150 years ago this place planted deep pain and hate in the hearts of both the Dakota and the Minnesota Settlers, however what we do this year can plant seeds for healing and reconciliation. I shared the thoughts I had envisioned with Peter Lengkeek, he encouraged me to speak with Jim Miller the ride founder. A few days later I caught-up with Jim in Washington DC where he had been visiting universities. Here are the suggestions for those wanting to witness and participate in the Ceremony on December 26.

Persons not involved in the memorial ride or run, but desiring to participate, please consider the following:

1. **DRESS APPROPRIATELY:** Wear dark colors as a sign of sorrow with a brightly colored scarf or arm band as a sign of hope. Also remember to arrive early (before 9 am to assure time to park and get into places) but PLEASE: Do NOT crowd around the Stone Buffalo as that area needs to be kept open for the riders.

2. **WALK in SOLIDARITY:** Persons desiring to demonstrate their sorrow for the past and solidarity with the riders should walk behind the horses to the memorial site. Those willing to walk the 2 miles from Land of Memories Park may meet there, or fall in line along the way after the riders pass along S. Riverfront Drive. (There is parking in the High School, Cub Foods, and other parking lots) If you are unable to walk, please wait near the library until after the horses and runners have arrived at the Buffalo and then move in closer.

3. **RETURN of REMAINS:** After the execution of the Dakota Warriors, the graves were raided by local citizens, including the Dr. Mayo. If you have artifacts or bones from the

Dakota 38 please bring them (wrapped in cloth and in a box) so they can be returned to family members. If you know of people holding bones or artifacts encourage them to bring them. Official tribal historians will be available to assure the remains are treated properly. Your help in this will be greatly appreciated.

4. **EAT in COMMUNITY:** Bring a Hot Dish or other food to share and join with the riders for a pot-luck meal following the ceremony. Additionally there is a need for people to help with serving of the meal and clean-up afterwards.

5. **DONATE:** The ride has significant costs for transportation, care of the horses and housing of the riders. Donations can be accepted on-line or on the day of the event.

It may seem like a *different* way to spend your vacation, you may feel *out of your comfort zone*, but you will be welcomed and your presence will be appreciated. We hope to see you around the Stone Buffalo in Mankato on the 26th.

Consider...

"the status quo will continue until we envision a new path and begin to walk in it.." Have you ever had the opportunity to buck the status quo? Was this based on vision or reaction? What is the difference?

What does solidarity mean to you? Does it demand something? How have you seen or lived-out solidarity?

Dakota 38+2 Memorial Ride Nears Mankato

24DEC

Yesterday the riders made their way to Fort Ridgely from a pasture near the Birch Coulee Battle site where we had kept the horses. The Dakota 38 + 2 Ride is now in the heart of where the War of 1862 was fought. After the initial attack on the Lower Agency, where food supplies were being withheld from the starving Dakota families, Little Crow led an attack on the Fort where a small contingency of troops were stationed.

A few weeks later the Dakota Warriors attacked a detachment of soldiers about 16 miles to the North West of the Fort at the Birch Coulee. Here, along the Minnesota River Valley, is the area that was promised as a homeland after the Dakota surrendered their traditional lands in the deceptive Treaty of Traverse des Sioux in 1851.

As the ride makes its way along the river valley, one can imagine an eerie silence hung over this river valley 150 years ago; the Dakota had either fled or been imprisoned, many were awaiting execution, all were facing exile. The settlers had also fled; most were waiting for spring to return. Sorrow was palatable in the burned-out buildings and rotting corpses of horses that had been left from the battles.

To expand on the often quoted phrase,"An injustice against one, is an injustice against all" the aftermath of this short war was proof that, "the acceptance of injustice against any, will eventually impact all." A community that purports to support liberty cannot be sustained through injustice. Both the Civil War of the USA and this Civil War in Minnesota are proof of this truth.

I am unable to be with the riders during these days, responsibilities of work and family called me back to Minneapolis. Yet, while my body is not there, my mind and spirit are sill inextricably linked. I shared in a text message with a friend on the ride, "I still have sage in my pocket and songs in my heart".

Aided by text messages and the Facebook posts, the rhythm of the last 2 weeks continue to echo in my soul; first breakfast, then catch and load the horses, followed by morning circle and prayers, and then a day of 5 – 7 mile legs with fresh riders ready to take the staff and continue the ride at each interval. Finally, as the sunsets; closing circle and prayer, haul the horses to the corral, feed and water them, then head to supper, spend time talking and get ready for bed.

Christmas night I will return to prepare for the final leg, the ride into Mankato on the morning of the 26th; the place and the time when the 38 Dakota warriors died in the largest mass execution in US history. Please consider joining us there, to remember honor, and hopefully see healing and reconciliation in action.

Consider...

"A community that purports to support liberty cannot be sustained through injustice."

Does this saying also apply to smaller communities such as neighborhoods, schools, and churches?

What regular disciplines are required to keep injustice at a minimum within any community?

Silent Night, Holy Night; the Gallows are Ready for Brothers in Christ

25DEC

Last night I sat in a Christmas Eve service with my family. It was a beautiful service but my mind kept straying out the window where the clear sky displayed a brilliant sunset. I knew my brothers in the Dakota 38+2 ride were wrapping up the day, praying, and feeding the horses. My imagination took me from the corral in Cortland today to the prison in Mankato 150 years ago.

I thought of the story we had heard along the ride of the police chief in Madison SD. Last year, he shared from a journal of his grandfather's, who had guarded both the 38 awaiting death in Mankato and those who were later sent to prison in Davenport IA. In his journal it was clear that these Dakota men had become his friends even as he was their guard. The Madison Chief of Police went on to explain how that had been an issue of shame for some of the family; "how could anyone befriend these savages?" But for the police chief, it was a matter of pride that his grandfather could see beyond prejudice and fear into a place of friendship.

Thinking about this particular family, I wondered to myself, "how many of those who crowded around the gallows on the 26th of December, also crowded around the manger scene the day before?" What was on the mind of those parishioners as they contemplated the coming of the "Prince of Peace" while they simultaneously planned and prayed for the execution of many, and the exile of all, the Dakota from Minnesota? To me this is one of the most shameful aspects of the causes and the results of this conflict. While many Americans like to claim we are a "Christian Nation," there was *nothing* in the overall narrative between the relationships of Minnesota and the Dakota that reflect the teachings of Jesus Christ.

Most of the Dakota who were executed were baptized Christians, many of them were guilty of nothing more than going to "just war" as defined by Christian theology. The majority of the Dakota never took up arms against their oppressor, *yet all were exiled.* Many of the Dakota had embraced the Gospel and become Christians, *yet this meant nothing to a people who wanted the land to themselves.* Regardless of a shared faith, the prejudice of culture and color would not allow the white settles to see the Dakota as true brothers. True, acts of terror were committed by Dakota warriors. However, by comparison they are far eclipsed in both scope and scale by the terror inflicted on the Dakota by Minnesotans and the US government before and after this uprising.

As the Warriors went to the gallows they sang a song. A Dakota Hymn, a Christian Hymn, written by Joseph Renville in 1842. The song is titled "Wankantanka Taku Titawa" or "Many and Great, O God are your Works, Maker of Earth and Sky."

The second verse they sang takes on powerful meaning considering nooses are being put over their concealed heads.

> *Grant unto us communion with you, O star abiding One; Come into us and dwell with us; with you are found the gifts of life. Bless us with life that has no end, eternal life with you.*

As we spend Christmas night with our families, may we consider what reconciliation and the true message of Christmas really requires of us.

While that concludes the blog messages I wrote, this in no way concludes my thoughts, nor this journey that has begun. I returned to Minneapolis to begin an enormous job that awaited Minne-Mex Construction. Evenings and weekends have been consumed by work with our crew of Latino and Native American workers.

However relationships begun on the ride have continued to grow through visits, Facebook, and phone calls. My awareness to various issues has been heightened, my sensitivities sharpened in unique ways. One thing I know for sure; a journey that began in personal study, led to corporate actions which created new relationships and contexts of awareness, has resulted in personal transformation and glimpses of Beloved Community along the way.

Consider...

How do personal convictions or faith beliefs impact the way you think of your "enemy"?

Have your friendships and convictions ever cost you "social capital"? How?

Do you think it is accurate for Marque to say, "While many Americans like to claim we are a "Christian Nation," there was nothing in the overall narrative between the relationships of Minnesota and the Dakota that reflect the teachings of Jesus Christ."

Why or why not?

Has personal study ever opened doors to new convictions and relationships in your life?

Bleached of the struggle

Bleached of the fight

Sanitized Crucifix all pasty white

Half the nutrients

Yet easy to digest

A white-bread Jesus

Held hostage by the west

Bleached of the struggle

Bleached of the fight

Sanitized Crucifix all pasty white

Historically Inaccurate

A potent social curse

The colonizing messiah

Put millions in the hearse

Son of peasant-farmer-pioneer stock on the prairie,

Bible/flag theology was my burden to carry.

Taught that the doctrine of Manifest Destiny,

Gave divine right to everything west of me.

WASP theology really ain't ALL wack -

But will blame God's sovereignty when Justice is lack.

The risen, prince of peace - not doctrines - west or east,

ushers in salvation and drives out the beast.

Bleached of the fight

Sanitized Crucifix all pasty white

Half the nutrients

Yet easy to digest

A white-bread Jesus

Held hostage by the west

Bleached of the struggle

Bleached of the fight

Sanitized Crucifix all pasty white

Historically Inaccurate

A potent social curse

The colonizing messiah

Put millions in the hearse

Millions walk away reject the stain–glass fake!

A god of race-based nationalized easy-take.

Capitalist theology – optional compassion

Their bottom-line dictates social action.

But we cannot deny across time and space

The real brown Jesus brings peace and grace

He a friend of sinners, not political elite

He's the Reconciler, liberator,

On the justice seat

Postlogue

I am NOT sure of many things in this messy, but necessary, journey to Beloved Community. But I am sure that the journey is the purpose. You *never* fully arrive in community; you *never* are totally reconciled with any other human. Conflict and re-injury are as much a part of the relationship as breathing is to life.

Yet, we can commit to remain on the path, to engage those around us, to invite those forgotten. Sometimes it is weary, and seems as if every day is about identifying injury and seeking forgiveness. But that is the example we have been given. 'While we were yet sinners, Christ died for us."

I invite you to stay on the road, or perhaps get out of the ditch. Find others to join you in the conversation in making your journey to Beloved Community.

Marque Jensen

Let Justice Roll Down

www.mmjmpls.org

SPECIAL THANKS TO THE FOLLOWING
WHO KICKED IN @ KICKSTARTER:

Fellow Sojourners:		**Group Journey Guides:**
Amy and Bob Mingo	Margo Allen-Hurst	Lorie Crandall
Rob Brock	Vida Kent	Dawn Stolee
Ariah Fine	Traci Moore	Neeraj Mehta
John LeMay	Marlon Haverdink	Tub Jason Yang
Jeremy Scheller	Trevor Tungseth	Dave and Pam Bolin
Cheryl Anderson	Tammy Norlin	Elise and Tony Probasco
Michelle and Victor Muthiani	Ron Archer	Deb and Dennis White
Michelle Perkins	Matthew Spillum	Paula and Jared Cox
Curtiss DeYoung	Ruth Picker	Jonathan Rangoonwala
Brian Mogren	Jennifer Lachermeier	Urban Homeworks
Roxxanne Obrien	Jake Martens	
Dee McIntosh	Kyle Dick	
Laura Woody	Richard Matson Daley	
Kyle Norell	Stephen Chu	
Jennifer Pins	Sierra Asamoa-Tutu	
C. John Hildebrand	Veann Beutler	
Bryan and Terri McAnnay	Laura Mastbergen	
	Lynn and Dan Bolin	

Interested in taking a next step in the journey? Consider becoming an Urban Neighbor...

Living as an Urban Neighbor means living a life where faith and action are inseparable. Love where you live, and live on purpose! Take your next steps in experientially understanding what role you have to play in the Beloved Community as an Urban Neighbor.

The Urban Neighbor Community is a faith-motivated, ministry-of-presence experience for college students and working professionals. Urban Neighbors have the opportunity to experience mutually liberating relationships as they seek to know, understand, enrich and be enriched by the hope that exists in the urban contexts of Minneapolis and Saint Paul.

Urban Neighbors Commit To:

Serve. Volunteer 2-3 hours weekly with a local ministry or organization that is already acting as a tool within the urban community.

Learn. Join with other Urban Neighbors monthly to intentionally learn about life and ministry, justice and mercy in the urban context from community leaders.

Live. Gather regularly with housemates as you go deeper in following Jesus together in the city.

The experience will change your life and give you a new perspective on what it means to truly be a neighbor. Find out more by visiting www.urbanhomeworks.org/housing/urban-neighbors

CPSIA information can be obtained at www.ICGtesting.com
Printed in the USA
LVOW07s0022050814

397487LV00005B/13/P